IT'S OUR TURN NOW

MARIO MURILLO

**CHARISMA
HOUSE**

Visit the author's website at mariomurillo.org.

Cataloging-in-Publication Data is on file with the Library of Congress.
International Standard Book Number: 978-1-63641-145-3
E-book ISBN: 978-1-63641-146-0

While the author has made every effort to provide accurate internet addresses at the time of publication, neither the publisher nor the author assumes any responsibility for errors or changes that occur after publication. Further, the publisher does not have any control over and does not assume any responsibility for author or third-party websites or their content.

23 24 25 26 27 — 987654321
Printed in the United States of America

Author's note: I have chosen to capitalize Woke and Wokeness to show that it is a formal religion.

CONTENTS

PART IV: FINISHING STRONG

INTRODUCTION

A GOLDEN OPPORTUNITY IS churning amid America's moral and physical disaster. The call from God is clear and strong: "Come and let Me make you fit to seize this golden opportunity." The Spirit of God is telling us it is our turn now.

Political, corporate, and media villains have had their day and their say. It is our turn now.

It is our turn now because the misery caused by the Left and Wokeness will ignite the largest influx of conversions to Christ we have seen in our lifetime. The billions of dollars spent to erase the Christian faith will prove to be an utter waste. We are entering a season where Christian influence in America will greatly increase.

He who holds power to reverse plots, make plans backfire, and cause the wrath of man to boomerang has been quietly working. Soon His handiwork will be revealed. It is a massive harvest of souls that are being ripened by misery, corruption, and tyranny. How do I know this is true? Because I have already seen it.

I wrote this book because something shocking and unexplainable started happening in our tent crusades. At the height of a pandemic lockdown—in California, the bluest state in America—thousands were being converted to Christ.

You can barely get Californians to a Christian meeting when it is *convenient*. But then they started coming during a lockdown. It filled me with questions: Why were they overflowing the tent now that leaving their house was almost impossible? What was happening? Why was it happening?

It's our turn now. That phrase kept repeating in my heart. It was a clue of some kind. The feeling kept growing within that I would witness some great event. Then the scales fell off my eyes.

I realized that as glorious as our tent crusades are, they are only a small part of a great and widespread phenomenon brewing nation-wide. That is why I believe there is an urgent warning from the throne of God to get ready for harvest.

The church has been through so much these last few years. The last thing we need is a book that raises false hopes. This book's message is not another case of prophetic wishful thinking about some future event. This is happening now.

Yes, evil is exalted in America. Yes, it looks bad for the church. Indeed, those who control the teleprompters have a clear message: "Christians have no place in the America we are building. You are not wanted—and soon you will be discarded."

But listen to Jesus in John 4:35: "Do you not say, 'There are still four months and then comes the harvest'? Behold, I say to you, lift up your eyes and look at the fields, for they are already white for harvest!"

Jesus is telling anyone who will listen that the harvest is now. Do not think more must happen before we harvest souls. Do not look at the frightening pictures. Look with spiritual eyes to the fields. The images of hatred and rejection do not tell the real story. You can see something wonderful if you look beyond the stage props.

My claim that leftists and atheists are setting us up for a harvest of souls is not a knee-jerk outburst; it is a settled conviction. The evidence is all around us. There is no need to set the thermostat to hyperemotional. There is no need to embellish this book with buzzwords or play the "God told me" card to get the point across.

I do not want to make a motivational speech. I want to make an airtight case. I will show you why all the armies in the world cannot stop a vessel of God whose time has come.

DISCERNING THE TIMES

In the first section of this book, you will see what is happening right now. I'll explain why America is at an extraordinary place, with insight that goes deeper than what you will get through other sources. You will understand the times. You will grasp the lead-up to the great harvest.

Fear grips a weary nation. Dreadful questions crash into us like angry waves. How can America recover from the ravages of the last few years? Can any nation survive the multiple lashes of a pandemic, an avalanche of perversion, and total division, violence, and hatred?

What about the devastation planned by megabillionaires? Did a handful of villains who own much of the planet orchestrate these calamities to beat America into global submission? If they shackle us in their chains, will we ever escape? No nation that has lost its freedom has ever regained it.

These are harsh questions, but the real question we should be asking is this: What if the things we fear most are creating the perfect climate for mass conversions to Christianity?

We will take a fresh look at Elijah on Mount Carmel. His story will come alive, revealing that his actions toward Ahab, Jezebel, and the utterly depraved condition of Israel are the model for our actions today.

I pray that before you finish the first section, you will make an irrevocable commitment to let God use you in the greatest way you have ever known.

THE HARVEST IS NOW

In section 2, you will see the factors and forces that are ripening vast fields of human souls. There's a biblical model for this as well. Paul's arrest shook the church to its core. It looked like a checkmate for the church. Then something strange happened. He wrote, "I want to report to you, friends, that my imprisonment here has had the opposite of its intended effect. Instead of being squelched, the Message has actually prospered" (Phil. 1:12, MSG).

The only way an attack can have the opposite of its intended effect is for the enemy weapon to be intercepted, to be overpowered, and to backfire on *them*. As Esther 7:10 says, "So they hanged Haman on the gallows that he had prepared for Mordecai."

The global gallows these masters of war are building will also be appropriated. God is laughing at them.

> Why do the nations rage, and the people plot a vain thing? The kings of the earth set themselves, and the rulers take counsel together, against the LORD and against His Anointed, saying, "Let us break Their bonds in pieces and cast away Their cords from us."
>
> He who sits in the heavens shall laugh; the Lord shall hold them in derision. Then He shall speak to them in His wrath, and distress them in His deep displeasure: "Yet I have set My King on My holy hill of Zion."
>
> —PSALM 2:1–6

YOUR UNIQUE ROLE

Section 3 will train you to bring in the harvest. I want these pages to instill rock-solid hope and encouragement in you. I want each chapter to answer burning questions and provoke you to true greatness in a dark world. Most of all, I want this section to prepare you for your unique role in what I believe is the best thing God has ever done for America.

You will see the *who, what, where,* and *when* of soul winning. You will understand why you belong at the table of influence. You will confirm your identity as a destroyer of the devil's works.

The work of the Holy Spirit is to envelop the earth with the conviction of sin, righteousness, and judgment. This is now happening in America. The Holy Spirit is deeply working on hearts. To bring in the harvest, we must quit doing things our way and surrender to the ongoing master plan of God's harvest.

Think about it. The prayer Jesus prescribed was this: "The harvest truly is plentiful, but the laborers are few. Therefore pray the Lord of the harvest to send out laborers into His harvest" (Matt. 9:37–38).

If they had to be sent to the harvest, it means these laborers were somewhere else and had to be called into the harvest. So where were they? And what were they doing?

OUR TRIUMPH IS GUARANTEED

Section 4 will show you how to finish strong. The stage is set. The conditions are right. The masses are ready, and God is turning hearts back to Him. But one last, fearful enemy remains. The threat that can cheat us from knowing the hour of our visitation is the killer frost that would have us sleep through the harvest.

What is this hideous monster? The beast within us is the dark thing that has our eyes glued to the images of our depraved culture so that the seeming impossibility of victory would freeze us in our tracks.

The Holy Spirit is walking right up to you and shaking you free. He is telling you that the cruel enemy does not matter. The lack of soldiers does not matter. The money does not matter. Your level of talent does not matter.

Only one thing matters. Only one thing guarantees our triumph. There is an irresistible and irrepressible reason we will win big. God has spoken and told us why we will win: because it's our turn now.

Evil, you have had your day. The God haters have had their say. The tyrants have had their way. But it's our turn now.

PART I:

WHAT'S HAPPENING

In this section I'll discuss what is happening in America now. By understanding the times and where we are headed, you will know what to do and why to do it.

PART 1

WHAT'S HAPPENING

Chapter 1

IT'S OUR TURN NOW

I T'S YOUR TURN. You may not know it. You may not believe it. But it is your turn. And it is not just any kind of turn. This one is dangerous, and the odds against it are astronomical.

Nevertheless, I strongly believe that you will take your turn. What will convince you? When all the facts are in—and you see what will happen if you do not act—you will take your turn. And when you see the power and the glory of taking your turn, you not only will lose your fear of taking your turn; you will yearn to take it.

How did I learn the power of taking your turn? The lesson did not come to me in church and had nothing to do with preaching. It came on a jet plane and had everything to do with baseball.

A CONVERSATION I'LL NEVER FORGET

It was a situation only God could orchestrate. For ten years a baseball question haunted me, and only one person in the entire world could answer it for me. Then one day, though there's an average of forty-five thousand daily airline flights worldwide, he walked onto my flight. And the seat next to him stayed open.

Tommy Lasorda, the legendary manager of the Los Angeles Dodgers, took a seat in the row in front of me. I knew I must ask him a question—a question about *that moment*.

Was it the most electrifying moment in the history of sports? Millions believe so. It was October 15, game 1 of the 1988 World Series between the Oakland Athletics and the Los Angeles Dodgers.

Of course, it came down to the bottom of the ninth inning. And of course, there were two outs, with the Dodgers down by one run.

The Dodgers should not have been there. The year before, 1987, they finished seventeen games behind the division-winning San Francisco Giants. But in 1988, after improbably winning the National League West, they faced the New York Mets in the National League Championship Series.

This time their chances were not just improbable; they were extremely improbable. The Mets had compiled an impressive 100–60 (.625) regular-season record. But the most devastating statistic was this: the Dodgers had played the Mets eleven times in the regular season and lost ten times.

Somehow they found a way to beat the Mets in seven games. But it cost them their star player, Kirk Gibson, who sustained injuries to both legs. He hurt his left hamstring stealing second base in game 5, and he hurt his right knee in game 7. He was out of the World Series.

In spite of this loss, the Dodgers had home-field advantage and started game 1 of the World Series strong, scoring two runs in the first inning. But a second-inning grand slam by Jose Canseco put the Oakland A's ahead, seemingly for good.

At one point, as the Dodgers had trailed for several innings, TV cameras scanned their dugout, and NBC's Vin Scully commented that Gibson was "nowhere to be found." Unknown to fans and media, Gibson was watching the game from the Dodgers' clubhouse while undergoing physical therapy.

Scully's words ignited Gibson. With the assistance of batboy Mitch Poole, Gibson told Tommy Lasorda that he was available to pinch-hit in the ninth inning and immediately went to the batting cage in the clubhouse to take practice swings.

Now we come to the bottom of the ninth. The Dodgers were losing by one run and down to their last out when Lasorda made the insanely courageous decision to let Gibson bat.

Suddenly, Kirk Gibson started walking to the plate. A deafening roar broke out in Dodger Stadium, and Vin Scully proclaimed, "And look who's coming up! All year long, they looked to him to light the fire, and all year long, he answered the demands until he was physically unable to start tonight—with two bad legs: the bad left hamstring and the swollen right knee. And, with two out, you talk about a roll of the dice, this is it."

Gibson immediately fouled off two pitches. The count was 0–2. He swung clumsily and dribbled the next pitch foul down the first-base line, confirming his inability to swing with any power. Gibson took an outside pitch, and it was ruled a ball by home plate umpire Doug Harvey. Then he fouled off a pitch and took another outside pitch to work to a 2–2 count. The seventh pitch was a ball, making it a full count.

Then, swinging almost entirely with his upper body, Gibson sent the next pitch over the right-field fence. The incredible hit was narrated by Vin Scully: "High fly ball into right field. She is gone! In a year that has been so improbable, the impossible has happened."

Gibson limped around the bases and pumped his fist as his teammates stormed the field. The Dodgers won game 1 with a score of 5–4. For almost two minutes, Vin Scully said nothing, letting the crowd's roar do all the talking.[1]

It was the shot heard around the world.

So there I was, sitting right behind Tommy Lasorda on a flight to Los Angeles. The seat belt sign went off, and I was free to roam about the cabin. The seat next to him was empty. I introduced myself. He was very gracious, and we began an unforgettable conversation.

Eventually we reached the point where I could ask my burning question about *that moment*. "Tommy, I must ask you a question. Why did you let Kirk Gibson pinch-hit?"

What he said next still reverberates in me. "Mario, *I knew it was his turn.*"

What that moment was to Kirk Gibson, this moment is to you, me, and the church. I know it's our turn!

Don't Miss Your Moment

Go back to that moment when Gibson was getting physical therapy in the clubhouse. How utterly unfair it must have seemed. He had an amazing season, only to lose out right at the finish line. Think how final his situation must have felt. He could have been drowning in his feelings. And if those feelings had won, he would have missed the greatest moment of his life. What a thought!

He didn't know he had one more turn in him, that even as injured as he was, there was still one more try. He found it when he heard Vin Scully say, "Kirk Gibson is nowhere to be found." That lit the fire—the same fire Gibson had lit in the Dodgers all season.

Gibson woke up. He realized that no matter how hobbled he was, he would have a lifetime to heal. But he only had this one moment, this one shot at immortality that would quickly pass and be gone forever. And the pain of missing this moment became greater than the pain in his body.

This is what I meant when I told you when all the facts are in—and you see what will happen if you do not act—you will take your turn.

What will it take for you and me to wake up and take our turn? What will it take for you to reject the impossibility of this time? We stand in a far more important place than any professional athlete.

A lot of people—including Gibson's wife—made the mistake of leaving Dodger Stadium early. They left because they believed it was a lost cause. Imagine hearing on the radio that you just missed perhaps the greatest home run in baseball history. That was their great mistake. But you and I can make a far worse mistake.

We can miss the greatest miracle God has ever done for America because we think it is a lost cause. We have far greater motivation than baseball. We have an infinitely greater legacy than a World Series.

It stung Gibson's soul to hear that he was nowhere to be found. But right now heaven is glancing into the main arena and saying of us, "They are nowhere to be found." You and I can come up with all kinds of excuses for being MIA but not one good reason.

Consider the movement you belong to. I don't mean the make-believers, lukewarm to the bone, who traipse in and out of religious edifices. I am talking about the core. I mean those who remember that they come from a family of giant-killers and lion-tamers.

The memory of Christian heroes haunts us. It provokes us. It reminds us how wrong it is to fear and hunker down and hide. Everything about Christian history demands that we stand, believe, and take our shot at immortality. It's our turn now.

How could Kirk Gibson have imagined what would happen next? Consider the extremes. At one moment, he has given up on a dream. The next moment, he is limping around the bases in the highest glory a ballplayer can know. That is the power of an inner spark that drives a person to try one more time. That is what I am begging you to do.

And consider the adversity Gibson faced—the veritable impossibility of the situation. That is what deepened the glory. That fact must pervade our spirits when we are in the heat of battle.

No One Can Make You Take Your Turn—Except You

You must speak to your own soul. You must take authority over it. Tell it, "America is in agony. But this agony will only heighten the glory God will receive when our national miracle arrives."

All the malignant darkness, perversion, and hatred consuming America can be crushed beneath our feet. Every doubt and fear can be replaced by a supernatural resolve to volunteer for battle.

Lasorda could not force Gibson to risk his body. Gibson had to volunteer. You too must volunteer. Psalm 110:3 (AMP) says, "Your people will offer themselves willingly [to participate in Your battle] in the day of Your power." Look closely. The volunteers did not create the power. The power—the day of power—created the volunteers.

I told you that I believe you will take your turn. Now the power of God is pulling on you. It is pushing you to stand. It is provoking deep passion in you.

Will you take the next step? Move into something magnificent. Start your training.

And now meet Elijah the prophet. Elijah will now be our guide and role model. Whereas Kirk Gibson defeated a man on the mound, Elijah defeated 450 prophets of Baal on a mountain. Kirk Gibson fired the shot heard round the world, and Elijah called down an explosion of fire that has reverberated for thousands of years. He will show us how to take our turn.

Chapter 2

ELIJAH, THE ASTONISHING EXAMPLE

I F EVER A man loved God and his country, it was Elijah. It broke his heart to see wickedness disfigure the great nation of God. When Elijah took his turn, it was something truly astonishing to behold. He was handpicked. Not only did Elijah know it was his turn, but he also knew how to take his turn as well as anyone in the Old Testament.

The fire that Elijah prayed down on Mount Carmel ranks as one of the greatest displays of supernatural power the world has ever witnessed.

> "Hear me, O LORD, hear me, that this people may know that You are the LORD God, and that You have turned their hearts back to You again." Then the fire of the LORD fell and consumed the burnt sacrifice, and the wood and the stones and the dust, and it licked up the water that was in the trench. Now when all the people saw it, they fell on their faces; and they said, "The LORD, He is God! The LORD, He is God!" And Elijah said to them, "Seize the prophets of Baal! Do not let one of them escape!" So they seized them; and Elijah brought them down to the Brook Kishon and executed them there.
>
> —1 KINGS 18:37–40

This intervention was extreme and violent. The situation demanded it. Israel had debased itself beyond recognition.

For the singular task of saving Israel, God chose an amazing man.

Elijah is one of the greatest men in the Bible. The great English minister and Bible commentator Matthew Henry wrote,

> He only, of all the prophets, had the honour of Enoch, the first prophet, to be translated, that he should not see death, and the honour of Moses, the great prophet, to attend our Saviour in his transfiguration. Other prophets prophesied and wrote, he prophesied and acted, but wrote nothing; but his actions cast more lustre on his name than their writings did on theirs.[1]

An entire nation backing 450 prophets of Baal getting ready to blaspheme God on Mount Carmel is the perfect parallel to our crisis. Elijah is the perfect example of how God forges a man or woman for His purposes and then prepares them. He trained Elijah on how to take his turn and when to take it.

But the task assigned to Elijah was far more perilous than we can imagine. He walked into the gates of hell, for indeed Israel was a living hell. A thousand times his life was threatened, and a thousand times he refused to defect to Baal.

As Americans, we know what it is like to languish under a corrupt government. We can all think of politicians who have abused their power to degrade and contaminate every vestige of American life. Because of their influence, evil is exalted and righteousness is hated.

We must contend with those in power the way Elijah had to contend with Ahab and Jezebel. "But there was no one like Ahab who sold himself to do wickedness in the sight of the LORD, because Jezebel his wife stirred him up" (1 Kings 21:25). Jezebel had filled the vat with the grapes of wrath.

Elijah walked into a place where Jezebel had erased God. She had cursed the Promised Land. She had enslaved the righteous and exalted the vile. She had killed all the prophets except those hidden in caves. There seemed to be no way to stop her. But that is precisely what Elijah was called to do.

God's Heart for America

Elijah began with the burden of the Lord. He carried it. He lived and breathed it. In the following chapters we will see that our effectiveness begins with seeing God's heart for our nation. He does not want to put a bandage on the problem. He wants to root out the wickedness. He wants one nation under God. Elijah knew what he had to do, and so must we.

Elijah told Ahab that he had brought misery upon the people of Israel. (See 1 Kings 18:18.) Having God's heart means we see the misery of our nation. But we also see how this misery is ripening souls for a mass harvest. Everything we've been experiencing in America is leading to a great backfire! The very things we think are obstacles are catalysts for God to display His power. Those things we consider setbacks are fuses for an awakening.

Evil feels so permanent and powerful—until God turns off the water. Experiencing three and a half years of drought was a total game changer for Israel. Baal was a god they trusted to bring rain. Jehovah shamed him from the jump. The drought humbled and broke the people to the point that they began questioning Baal.

We must remember that the evils in the land are mere stage props, and whoever carries God's heart also carries His power.

> And Elijah the Tishbite, of the inhabitants of Gilead, said to Ahab, "As the LORD God of Israel lives, before whom I stand, there shall not be dew nor rain these years, except at my word."
> —1 KINGS 17:1

Elijah did not make this declaration of a drought in a corner. He went straight to the king. The king had the power to make the nation repent. We cannot hide because we fear tyrants. We are to prophesy in their courts and under their porches.

We cannot let evil politicians assign us any role in society beneath our calling. Tear off the labels they try to put on you. We are not racists, Nazis, deplorables, or any other lies with which they try to brand us. We belong in the halls of power. We have a right to rebuke and declare!

God Will Turn the Tables

As you go deeper into this book, I will show you how we can turn the tables on the enemy. In the Old Testament, Elijah took everything Ahab and Jezebel threw at him and threw it right back. We can find a New Testament model for this as well.

> But before all these things, they will lay their hands on you and persecute you, delivering you up to the synagogues and prisons. You will be brought before kings and rulers for My name's sake. But it will turn out for you as an occasion for testimony. Therefore settle it in your hearts not to meditate beforehand on what you will answer; for I will give you a mouth and wisdom which all your adversaries will not be able to contradict or resist.
> —Luke 21:12–15

It will turn! It will look as if you are doomed, but the situation will be turned to your advantage. You will be given words—irresistible words that will silence them!

Paul experienced this in prison and wrote about it in Philippians 1:12: "But I want you to know, brethren, that the things which happened to me have actually turned out for the furtherance of the gospel."

I love *The Message* Bible translation of this verse: "I want to report to you, friends, that my imprisonment here has had the opposite of its intended effect. Instead of being squelched, the Message has actually prospered."

Paul said his imprisonment had the opposite of its intended effect! I will show you how evil's attacks on us will boomerang back onto it.

Elijah stood with clear authority. Read again what Elijah said to Ahab: "As the LORD God of Israel lives, before whom I stand, there shall not be dew nor rain these years, except at my word" (1 Kings 17:1).

Elijah was saying, "The rain will stop at my command. It will not return until I say so." Elijah spoke with authority and declared that he and not the evil king had the authority, which the supernatural power of God displayed. In this dark time, the Lord will not give us simply irresistible words but signs and wonders that will confirm our words. A later chapter will focus on the right way to surrender and see signs and wonders.

So what if others have been false, arrogant, or greedy. We can be pure and faithful. Romans 3:3 (AMP) says, "What then? If some did not believe or were unfaithful [to God], their lack of belief will not nullify and make invalid the faithfulness of God and His word, will it?"

THE POWER OF BEING HIDDEN BY GOD

It took time for the drought to humble Israel. A withering drought began at the word of Elijah. But instead of fearing God, Ahab wanted to kill Elijah. So because they wanted to kill Elijah, God hid him.

The Left in America is exactly like that. They blame the church for the very social disasters they have caused. Like Elijah, we can learn the power of being hidden by God.

Elijah was a man of action. Waiting was probably the hardest thing God could ask him to do. He had to wait for the call to perform one of the most astounding acts of all time.

There are many urgent and powerful reasons for the wait. Sometimes we accomplish more than we can ever imagine in those times when we seem to be getting nowhere.

Jezebel was Elijah's greatest enemy, yet to show her what an empty threat she was, God found a hiding place for the man who prophesied her demise, even in her country.

Think of that! The place God had chosen for the prophet's

holding pattern was significant. Elijah was waiting in Zarephath, a city of Sidon outside the borders of the land of Israel. Sidon was where Jezebel came from. (See 1 Kings 16:31.) It was where the evil that plagued Israel was spawned. And here the miracle that freed Israel would be born.

Great vessels of God are tested by waiting in obscurity. God is doing a great work in you in your hiding place. The works God forces you to do in secret—without audience or fanfare—will lead to an open reward. (See Matthew 6:4.)

But there is still more being accomplished by Elijah's exile. He must learn anew that only God can do the miracle. And only God will get the glory. How utterly frustrating for Elijah to perform two amazing miracles and remain in hiding.

By the anointing of God, Elijah multiplies grain and oil for a widow—who ends up with an unlimited supply. But it did not become widely known. How is that possible?

A modern equivalent might be a gas station selling gasoline for fifty cents a gallon. The news would spread everywhere. Cars would be backed up for miles. In a famine, it could be even worse. News of any food source would spread like wildfire. People would race to the scene. But no one did.

Then there is the even greater miracle of her young son being raised from the dead. A resurrection? Are you kidding me? That would gather a massive crowd. Again, no one came.

To Elijah, this was frustrating. Surely the people needed to know he was working miracles. And just as surely the miracle power on display in Sidon would be better spent on saving Israel. Oh, the wisdom of God!

THE PURPOSE OF DIVINE FRUSTRATION

What was God doing to Elijah? Elijah may have wondered why the miracles did not lead to promotion. He was probably unaware of the greater miracle God was doing.

Remember, Ahab wanted Elijah dead. This prophet was a wanted man. No doubt, the king hired assassins to go and find him. Even with the miracles Elijah had performed, they could not find him. Matthew Henry said, "We left the prophet Elijah wrapt up in obscurity. It does not appear that either the increase of the provision or the raising of the child had caused him to be taken notice of at Zarephath, for then Ahab would have discovered him."[2] God was hiding him in plain sight.

Perhaps you feel like Elijah as you read this right now. You have seen mighty acts of God that did not grow your church or thrust you into a wider ministry. Why? God may be hiding you for your own protection. He protects us from success if it can destroy us. We do not want to take our turn before we are ready.

Until Jehovah forged Elijah's character to the point that he would not take the glory or be seduced by the glare of the national spotlight, he had to wait. And as Elijah waited, there was an even greater work to be done in him. God had to put fire in his belly. Elijah needed to become so intensely motivated that he would not just reach the finish line but blast across it.

Think of the heady situation he was about to face on the mountain. The king would be there. The 450 prophets of Baal would be there. All Israel would drop everything to see this confrontation, which would decide if Jehovah or Baal was God.

Elijah could not betray an iota of fear or intimidation. His voice could not crack; his faith could not flag. We do not even know if Elijah fully understood what he was about to do on Mount Carmel. So how did the Holy Spirit accomplish this in him? He did it by creating divine frustration.

Think of this when you feel you are going backward—away from your goal. Think of a bow and arrow. The arrow does not understand that to fly forward, it must first go backward. The arrow is going away from its destination, not toward it. The tension created by pulling back the bowstring will determine the arrow's velocity.

Elijah could have thought, "What am I doing here? This is not taking me where I need to go. This is pulling me away from my goal." Prophets scream and cry out when God intensifies their frustration.

> Then I said, "I will not make mention of Him, nor speak anymore in His name." But His word was in my heart like a burning fire shut up in my bones; I was weary of holding it back, and I could not.
>
> —JEREMIAH 20:9

This book will show you that your greatest frustrations become the fuel that launches you. It is the hand of God working that frustration into you so that the mightiest surge against evil will come out of you. Do you see it? Everything you have been through is fitting together. The pieces that were scattered are flying together into one living weapon. Your turn is coming. And when it does, you will be ready.

When the time was right, Elijah heard the message from God that he had yearned for. "And it came to pass after many days that the word of the LORD came to Elijah, in the third year, saying, 'Go, present yourself to Ahab, and I will send rain on the earth'" (1 Kings 18:1).

It wasn't just rain coming. It was fire! Look out, Ahab and Jezebel. Look out, prophets of Baal. The man who is about to meet you on Mount Carmel is ready. There is a terrifying authority in his step. There is lightning in his eyes. You have never seen the likes of him before. He is forged, he is relentless, and he will not stop until you are destroyed.

Look out, you villains in America. A new breed of believer is coming with the attributes of Christ. We are not just lambs but lions forged for such a time as this, perfectly suited to take our turn at destroying evil.

Are you ready to be trained? Then read on.

Chapter 3

WHERE, WHAT, AND HOW

W E NEED THE biggest miracle America has ever known.
Abraham Lincoln stood to address the nation in his
second inaugural speech. The Civil War was nearly
over, and he had been reelected president. We cannot fathom the
crushing burden or the Herculean task he faced.

This speech was given only forty-one days before his assassination. I believe it was his greatest speech—eclipsing even his famous
Gettysburg Address. Many expected a victory speech. The people
wanted Lincoln to spike the ball and shame the vanquished foe.
What they got was just the opposite. He told the nation that God
was judging them—all of them—for slavery.

> If we shall suppose that American slavery is one of those
> offenses which in the providence of God must needs come but
> which having continued through His appointed time He now
> wills to remove and that He gives to both North and South
> this terrible war as the woe due to those by whom the offense
> came shall we discern therein any departure from those divine
> attributes which the believers in a living God always ascribe
> to Him. Fondly do we hope—fervently do we pray—that this
> mighty scourge of war may speedily pass away. Yet, if God
> wills that it continue until all the wealth piled by the bonds-
> man's two hundred and fifty years of unrequited toil shall be
> sunk and until every drop of blood drawn with the lash shall
> be paid by another drawn with the sword as was said three
> thousand years ago so still it must be said "the judgments of
> the Lord are true and righteous altogether."[1]

He grieved like a father whose children had fought and killed each other. He told America that God used the war to purify it. He made no bones about what it would take to heal and rebuild: repentance.

The *New York Times* didn't like it. What else is new? An editorial in the *Times* read, "He makes no boasts of what he has done, or promises of what he will do. All that he does is simply advert to the cause of the war."[2]

And as usual, the *New York Times* got it wrong—very wrong.

We dare not get it wrong today. America's deep crisis is being seized by God again. And again, it is to purify us. It took courage to say that America had sinned by enslaving human beings. It was even braver to say that we were being judged for that sin. He soberly warned that God was righteous in all His ways.

It is chilling but urgent that we see that God is already judging America. That sobering realization is the only thing that can induce the proper level of urgency to take us in the right direction.

Lincoln presciently gave us the right direction while speaking at the Illinois Republican Convention on June 16, 1858, nearly three years before the war. He said, "If we could first know *where* we are, and *whither* we are tending, we could better judge *what* to do, and *how* to do it."[3]

Lincoln hit the mark when he said, "If we could first know *where* we are." So where are we versus where he was? We are in a very dark place indeed. We are bitterly divided. We have abandoned God. We face an evil that may be even greater than the Civil War.

Lincoln had the advantage of knowing who the enemy was. We, on the other hand, face a monster with tentacles that reach into every aspect of our lives. We can't even count our dead. We may never know the true extent of the pandemic's harmful effects on our elderly, our young people, and our children.

Those in power in our nation operate with arrogant impunity. They no longer hide their intentions. They use their power to destroy anyone perceived as an enemy of their agenda or who threatens their power.

The media is a malicious mouthpiece of these tyrants. The media has sold its soul to radicalism and will tell whatever lie it takes to protect its agenda.

What about our children? Woke leaders have made it clear that parents should not be in charge of their children's upbringing in our nation because the federal government has seized that role. I fear that teachers have turned into activists, classrooms have turned into indoctrination camps, and what was once education has turned into nothing more than government grooming.

And don't even get me started on whether we'll ever have free elections again! If our current leaders hang on to power in the next election, they will know they can take tyranny to the next level. At that point, everyone who has posted something on social media against Wokeness will be hunted down.

The next question Lincoln raised was, "Whither are we tending?" America is tending toward disaster. Blatant immorality consumes Americans. When alertness matters most, our citizens are in an immoral stupor. Their appetites are leading them into slavery.

America's rejection of God is audacious and fierce. Atheists and pagans control many of our seats of power. We are a culture guilty of murdering the innocent and lusting for the aberrant. We evicted God and then gorged on depravity. We even dared to call this enlightenment.

Millions of Americans are oblivious to their true condition. They are not part of an advancing culture but a growing addiction. They are blind to the tech billionaires—social drug dealers—making cattle out of them.

A large portion of the modern church adds to our national shame. The denial in the American church is as big a disaster as anything I have named. I see many in my own Spirit-filled camp with their heads in the sand.

This is not a time to wave the anointing like a magic wand to bring everything back to how it used to be. If we're honest, those old ways have helped bring us to this place of weakness, confusion, and fear. "The way it used to be" left preachers utterly unprepared for their churches to be locked down and now controlled.

DESTRUCTION OR CORRECTION?

Why doesn't God just destroy America? God knows we have been all but begging for it. This book is called *It's Our Turn Now.* But are we so far gone that it is too late? Will you and I even get a turn at saving our nation?

I prayed and asked God if He planned to destroy America. I heard no audible voice, but I got a strong impression. No, we will not be destroyed. But we will be judged.

I have no doubt that God is currently judging America. But there are two kinds of judgment. There is a judgment of final destruction. And there is a judgment of correction.

In Luke 19, Jesus told Jerusalem it was too late. The people had rejected a long string of warnings—a physical visit by the Son of God Himself—and they finally crucified Him. They were doomed.

> Now as He drew near, He saw the city and wept over it, saying, "If you had known, even you, especially in this your day, the things that make for your peace! But now they are hidden from your eyes. For days will come upon you when your enemies will build an embankment around you, surround you and close you in on every side, and level you, and your children within you, to the ground; and they will not leave in you one stone upon another, because you did not know the time of your visitation."
>
> —LUKE 19:41–44

Jesus' words came to pass with excruciating accuracy. The Roman destruction of Jerusalem in AD 70 still stands as one of the most brutal destructions of any city. The Romans took months to obliterate the city and end the Jewish State. Truly, not one brick was left on top of another. (See Matthew 24:2.)

Josephus, the ancient Jewish historian, was taken captive during this siege. He claims the legions of Rome killed more than one million Jews and forced ninety-seven thousand into slavery.[4] It was the end of the Jewish State.

Now let's look at the type of judgment that is correction: Israel under Ahab and Jezebel fell into total depravity. But instead of sending annihilation, God sent Elijah. This is a baffling mercy.

Matthew Henry even said, "One might have expected God would cast off a people that had so cast Him off; but, as evidence to the contrary, never was Israel so blessed with a good prophet as when it was so plagued with a bad king. Never was a king so bold to sin as Ahab; never was prophet so bold to reprove and threaten as Elijah."[5]

When Elijah took his turn at that defiled generation, the result was astounding. But the appearance of Elijah begins with judgment. Observe: even when a corrective judgment is not destructive, it is still devastating.

Elijah took authority. He declared a drought. Remember what he said to Ahab in 1 Kings 17:1: "As the LORD God of Israel lives, before whom I stand, there shall not be dew nor rain these years, except at my word." Elijah was saying, "Let me show you who is really in charge here. Expect no rain till you hear from me again."

Israel was forced to dry out like a drunkard in rehab. The fruitful land became a barren wilderness. Might God do the same to America? I think He has already begun.

God Will Bring America to Repentance

I believe God will allow painful things to happen to bring America to repentance. Think about the implications—it means that calamities will come to whatever extent God deems necessary for the nation's survival.

In Lincoln's second inaugural address, he warned about judgment falling on America. I believe judgment will begin in the corrupt church. The Lord is willing to uproot the churches built by human marketing. Do you think the sudden rash of megachurches collapsing in scandal is just random?

He will rain judgment on unrepentant media ministries that have perverted His purposes. He is even willing to bring secret sins into open shame. And why not? The very voices God called to rebuke the flood of evil instead collaborated with the enemy. They traded the Word of God for a marketing scheme.

Charles Spurgeon is often quoted as saying, "A time will come when instead of shepherds feeding the sheep, the church will have clowns entertaining the goats."[6] Whether it was Spurgeon who said this or someone else, it definitely predicted this day.

God is even willing to skip using this present generation of believers. If necessary, He will pass over us and wait for another generation who will obey Him.

The Lord of all nations is willing to humble America economically. He is willing to topple our wealth and humble us before the eyes of the world.

The big tech billionaires have essentially declared war on God, but even they are not safe from His wrath. No matter how powerful they seem, God's wrath can come in an instant and penetrate any barrier.

Here's a verse to haunt bloodthirsty billionaires:

> And I will say to my soul, "Soul, you have many goods laid up for many years; take your ease; eat, drink, and be merry." But God said to him, "Fool! This night your soul will be required of you; then whose will those things be which you have provided?"
>
> —LUKE 12:19–20

If necessary, nature and the land itself will rebel against us. Many environmentalists who think the earth loves them would find it ironic and shocking to learn that nature groans because of them. Romans 8:21–22 says, "...because the creation itself also will be delivered from the bondage of corruption into the glorious liberty of the children of God. For we know that the whole creation groans and labors with birth pangs together until now."

Even the animal kingdom can rise up against us. The king of Assyria tried to repopulate Israel with illegal aliens to eradicate the worship of Jehovah. Here's what happened:

> Then the king of Assyria brought people from Babylon, Cuthah, Ava, Hamath, and from Sepharvaim, and placed them in the cities of Samaria instead of the children of Israel; and they took possession of Samaria and dwelt in its cities. And it was so, at the beginning of their dwelling there, that they did not fear the LORD; therefore the LORD sent lions among them, which killed some of them.
>
> —2 KINGS 17:24–25

This shows that there was also something sacred about the land itself. Likewise, America is a land of covenant. Those who made the first settlement in America made a covenant. The roots of that covenant were written in England even before they set foot on Plymouth Rock. The Plymouth Rock Foundation says,

> The Pilgrims, while they were meeting secretly at Scrooby Manor in England (1606), ratified their church covenant as described by [William] Bradford: "They shook off this yoke of antichristian bondage, and as the Lord's free people joined themselves (by a covenant of the Lord) into a church estate, in the fellowship of the gospel, to walk in all His ways made known, or to be made known unto them, according to their best endeavors, whatsoever it should cost them." This church covenant, drawn up by themselves as instructed in the Bible, became the precursor to all other covenants.[7]

This covenant is just too strong. God can cause even the land to revolt against those who would break it.

Now back to Elijah. After the initial decree of judgment in Israel, God immediately sent Elijah into hiding. First Kings 17:2–3 says, "Then the word of the LORD came to him, saying, 'Get away from here and turn eastward, and hide by the Brook Cherith, which flows into the Jordan.'"

Hiding the mighty man of God is part of God's judgment on Israel. In his commentary, Matthew Henry writes,

> This was intended, not so much for his preservation, for it does not appear that Ahab immediately sought his life, but as a judgment to the people, to whom, if he had publicly appeared, he might have been a blessing both by his instructions and his intercession, and so have shortened the days of their calamity; but God had determined it should last three years and a half, and therefore, so long, appointed Elijah to abscond, that he might not be solicited to revoke the sentence, the execution of which he had said should be according to his word. When God speaks concerning a nation, to pluck up and destroy, he finds some way or other to remove those that would stand in the gap to turn away his wrath. It bodes ill to a people when good men and good ministers are ordered to hide themselves.[8]

Sincere ministers should take heart at this. When false preachers prosper and mighty vessels are hidden—when all the money, fame, and attention go to voices that are shallow, insincere, proud, and even false while good ministers languish in obscurity—it is judgment.

But when the time comes—and it is coming soon—heaven will release modern Elijahs. Right now they are hidden like Kirk Gibson in the clubhouse. But they are coalescing around one purpose: to snatch America from the jaws of death.

They think they are forgotten or overlooked. They see little point to their obscurity. They are in the place where God forges raw metal into a razor-sharp weapon. They will not break ranks. They will take none of the glory. Hell trembles at their approach.

The "nightclub churches" have no use for them. But they are perfect for this moment. It is a moment that America does not deserve and could never earn. It is humbling beyond words that God would extend this inexpressible mercy. We will get to take our turn.

The final part of Lincoln's advice: "We could then better judge what to do, and how to do it." That is exactly what this book will do. It will remove all doubt about *what* to do to take our turn and train you on *how* to do it.

I know a harvest is coming, but the idea of saving the nation from its moral disaster is quite another thing. We cannot focus only on the number of converts. We must forge onward to true revival. We do not dare stop short of all the preparation and training we need to accomplish a great and mighty visitation of God.

Chapter 4

HEADING IN THE RIGHT DIRECTION

Elijah was headed toward Ahab like an asteroid from space. He would crash into Baal worship and obliterate it. Ahab and Jezebel, as well as Baal and his 450 prophets, had no clue what was about to hit them.

No vessel of God in history was ever better prepared. No weapon was ever more poised to attack. Every muscle was taut with expectation. "Just say the word, Lord God," Elijah whispered as he gazed toward Mount Carmel. Elijah was a man of purpose. He was a man who knew his direction.

Now, I must ask you, Are you headed in the right direction? My friend, either you are directed or you are drifting. Lincoln wanted to know too.

Look at Lincoln's quote again: "If we could first know *where* we are, and *whither* we are tending, we could then better judge *what* to do, and *how* to do it."

"Whither we are tending" in modern terms means we had better know our true condition because we may be drifting toward disaster and not even realize it. It may be painful to know our true condition, but without the truth we are in grave danger, and there is simply no way we will do the right thing—the effective thing—against evil.

DIRECTED OR DRIFTING?

How do you and I know if we're headed in the right direction? The first way to tell is to ask yourself, "Why am I doing this?" Knowing why will tell you which way to go.

Elijah knew why. He had rehearsed the infamy of Ahab and Jezebel again and again. He mourned the misery of God's people. Their children were being sacrificed to idols. Everything good, decent, and beautiful had been disfigured. The drought had made them barely more than wild animals scraping to stay alive. Few devastations remove human decency faster than famine.

The passion to bring divine justice was burning a hole in Elijah. Finally, the moment he so desperately yearned for arrived. As we've read in 1 Kings 18:1, God told Elijah to go to King Ahab, and He would send the rain. So much is contained in that command. The prophet knew that if the rain returned, Baal's prophets were dead.

Is the same fire that was inside Elijah inside you? If not, are you still on the dark, cruel journey that godless leaders have forced on us for the last several years? Evil legislators have stolen so much from our lives. What a disgrace they have made of America. What a living hell they have made of our inner cities.

Take yet another look at America. We cannot be confused about why we vehemently oppose Wokeness—or the villains who forced it on us. Never forget what we have lost and the monstrous perversions they have unleashed. Then consider the evil intentions and bondage yet to come unless God provides a miracle.

Do you feel the fury yet? Are you a poised, razor-sharp weapon? Does every atom of your being say that American life must be cleansed of this leftist curse?

Can you match Elijah's intensity? Surely America has hundreds of sites like Mount Carmel. Are you yearning for the green light to take *your* mountain?

Why Elijah's Confrontation Is a Fitting Example

I chose Elijah as a role model because he fits perfectly in what we are facing. I target Baal worship because it is so similar to Wokeness. They are almost interchangeable. Let us look at the eerie similarities.

First, here is Dr. Peter Marshall's definition of Baal worship from his 1944 sermon "Trial by Fire":

> Materialism had a god, and his name was Baal. He offered to his devotees the things that human instincts crave. He was a god of the flesh. His priests encouraged the people to follow their natural inclinations. It was worship in indulgence, expressed in lust, and adored in selfishness. It had no inhibitions at all.[1]

Wokeness fits every syllable of this description. Woke folk and Baal worshippers have this in common: they blindly follow their god even when it proves to be a destructive myth. Let me remind you that one of the chief promises of Baal worship was rain, yet no one questioned why there was no rain! If Baal was so great, why didn't he overrule Elijah's declaration and send rain? Because Baal was powerless before our mighty God.

Even their starvation did not drive them to rethink their ways and return to God—they just kept sacrificing to Baal.

Woke ideologues never question why their grand scheme is such a spectacular failure. They must quickly turn their eyes away from logic and common sense. Otherwise they would see the disturbing truth about gun control, vaccine mandates, critical race theory (CRT), drag queens reading to children, men competing in sports events as women, and the grooming of children to change their gender while hiding it from their parents.

Wokesters have mastered the art of deflection. This is best demonstrated by the moment that Ahab saw Elijah in 1 Kings 18:17: "Then it happened, when Ahab saw Elijah, that Ahab said to him, 'Is that you, O troubler of Israel?'" The person causing all the trouble was calling the man with the answer the troublemaker.

This is the very definition of deflection. It's when you attack or blame another person rather than accept criticism or blame for your own actions. When someone deflects, they are trying to feel less guilty, avoid negative consequences, and blame others. The guilty person deflects their guilt onto the person who is accusing them or another person. Simply put, Ahab was blaming Elijah for what Ahab himself was doing.

But Elijah threw it right back at him, as we see in 1 Kings 18:18: "And he answered, 'I have not troubled Israel, but you and your father's house have, in that you have forsaken the commandments of the LORD and have followed the Baals.'"

We must do exactly that when the Woke mob creates a mess and then blames Christians. We must throw it right back at them. Nothing irks me more than hearing some wimpy preacher on a talk show. They side with Woke lies and apologize for things the church never did wrong—all so they will look virtuous.

Elijah shot back at the vile king Ahab and cast off all pretense of politeness and protocol in the face of illicit royalty. In essence, he was saying, "I do not bow to your wicked rule. You brought the curse; I bring the cure."

The new voices from God will not placate evil authorities. They won't worry about being branded unloving or rude. They are too deep in the anointing for such malarkey. They will point the finger of God at evildoers. And do you know what? America is so ready for that kind of Christian! That is what you must be!

Woke comparisons continue in verse 21: "And Elijah came to all the people, and said, 'How long will you falter between two opinions? If the LORD is God, follow Him; but if Baal, follow him.' But the people answered him not a word." Why couldn't they answer? Because no one had proved that Baal was real!

The tyrants keeping the national distraction of Wokeness alive are exactly like that. When you ask for proof, all you get is silence.

Or they tell you to follow the science. But they don't even know how to define what a woman is.[2] And they themselves do not follow the science when it doesn't fit their agenda.

Why should you and I follow the science? It's much more telling to follow the money!

The silence after Elijah's challenge proved that the Israelites were ambivalent about Baal. They were dabbling in both Baal and Jehovah.

Peter Marshall said, "But still, Israel was confused. The inheritances of the past, the early teachings of their parents were not forgotten. Something of conscience was not yet drugged, and they were confused and uneasy. They took a little of Jehovah, and a little of Baal."[3]

Israel was stuck between the living God, Jehovah, and the false god, Baal. The nation had not yet embraced Jezebel's brave new world. Later, God would tell Elijah about the seven thousand servants of God who had never bowed to Baal (1 Kings 19:18).

Likewise, most of America has not embraced the Woke agenda. Our nation is stuck in a twilight zone. We are undecided about whom to serve. Much of the gender bending of our youth is fad and peer pressure, and Woke reports of how many want this perversion are greatly exaggerated. True gender dysphoria is very rare. If Wokesters would "follow the science," they'd know that a 2016 article in the *Annual Review of Clinical Psychology* reported that fewer than one in ten thousand males and one in thirty thousand females experience gender dysphoria.[4]

That is why we must be ready to take our turn. We must do whatever it takes.

We have an enormous field that is white unto harvest in America. Just because people have been silenced by Woke tyranny does not mean they have been converted.

Elijah's phrase "if Baal" reinforces that no one has proved that Baal is real. Elijah is accusing Ahab and Jezebel of force-feeding Baal without any proof that he exists.

Likewise, Woke tyrants and their lackeys are force-feeding us the lie that we need to sexualize our children, even though there is no evidence that it will do them any good. And while we are at it, let's lie about American history. What's wrong with misrepresenting the facts if it is for the greater good?

All their promises that the new rules, new definitions of relationships, and new information restrictions will lead to a better world have proved to be catastrophic failures. If they believed in anything they were saying, they would stop censoring and lying. They would welcome equal time.

"If Baal is God, let's find out." There was simply no way Ahab and Jezebel wanted this contest on Mount Carmel. But the nation was so desperate for rain that the prophet was able to force a contest on them.

That is the same way we will get our turn now. National desperation will lift the ban on Christians.

But the eeriest comparison is the hatred of children. Baal normally required the sacrifice of children, often the firstborn male child, who was sacrificed by fire. Wokeness also believes in child sacrifice—but on an industrial scale.

Baal promised gratification if you threw your child into the fire. And if you listen to Planned Parenthood's promises to pregnant women, they sound very close to the promises Baalites offered those who sacrificed their children. On Bonfire.com you can buy a T-shirt that says "Abortion is magical." Please tell me, What magic is that?

When the draft of Justice Samuel Alito's opinion was leaked, declaring that the court was leaning toward overturning *Roe v. Wade*, the bonfire of rage was instant and widespread. Has any culture ever screamed this loudly to keep the savage power to kill its children? More than sixty million babies have been killed since the Supreme Court's 1973 decision to legalize abortion,[5] but it is not nearly enough for these modern Baal worshippers.

WOKENESS WILL SOON BE OBSOLETE

The trouble with using the word Woke is that it is tired and soon will be obsolete. Not long after this book comes out, attacking Woke will come off as tedious overkill. So this is my swan song for Woke. I used it freely in this chapter, knowing it would soon be tossed onto the trash heap of passé words.

Wokeness is collapsing under the weight of its own absurdity. The Woke leaders have been outed as money-hungry fakes. Their spokespeople have invented silly words. Referring to mothers as "birthing persons" or anyone as "nonbinary" or complaining that peanut butter is implicitly racist is a cringey stretch. All these banalities are begging to be expunged from civilized culture.

And it is already turning. Remember when corporations thought it would make them look good to be Woke? They poured money into movements that utterly embarrassed them.

The Walt Disney Company bit the poisonous apple. Then it "Woke" up in a coma that found it banning the terms *boys* and *girls*.[6] It said it decided to declare war on parents' rights by backing a crusade to teach five-year-old children everything about LGBTQ+, including gay sex.[7]

You may have noticed I've capitalized Woke and Wokeness throughout this book. That's because I consider it to be a religion. And it is the most judgmental religion in America. We're told, "You can't say this, and you can't say that. You can't even think it." In Woke world, people can stop you and force you to address them with their own list of bizarre pronouns.

Woke government is doing nothing about what is really hurting you and your family. It caters to the screaming bullies who pose as victims.

Americans have grown weary of these people. They have had it with lockdowns, indoctrination of their children, and the constant whining and complaining from people who have been blessed to live in the greatest nation on earth.

Wokeness has made Americans miserable. Wokeness has drained the color out of everything beautiful, innocent, and meaningful. The things they gave us are sad and vile substitutes for the goodness they took away.

But Wokeness is opening the greatest door for the church in our lifetime—an opportunity beyond words. But I don't believe it is an opportunity for everyone in the church. A vast number of Christians are not ready, do not want to be ready, and will never be ready in time for an American confrontation on Mount Carmel.

This door in America will not be open long. We have reached a key moment that may never come again. The Lord does not need a lot of people for this miracle. Only one Elijah stood against 450 prophets of Baal. But if God is for us, who can be against us?

The drought in Israel led to a severe famine. This also opened a door. God's timing with Elijah was perfect. The climactic meeting between the prophet and the evil king was when Elijah dropped the gauntlet and challenged Ahab to a confrontation between two deities: Jehovah and Baal.

And then Elijah did something astounding in 1 Kings 18:19: "Now therefore, send and gather all Israel to me on Mount Carmel, the four hundred and fifty prophets of Baal, and the four hundred prophets of Asherah, who eat at Jezebel's table."

Elijah's challenge? He was saying: "The tables have turned. You have called your meetings. Now I am calling God's meeting. I want the whole crew. I demand a confrontation. You had your chance. You have had your day. It's our turn now! You have shown how miserable and perverted you can make a nation. You are bankrupt. You are a total failure. You have had more time than you should have. Your time is up. It's our turn now!"

The stage was set on Mount Carmel. The players were in place. Elijah told the false prophets to go first. And when they did, it resulted in their great humiliation. Verses 27–29 tell us:

And so it was, at noon, that Elijah mocked them and said, "Cry aloud, for he is a god; either he is meditating, or he is busy, or he is on a journey, or perhaps he is sleeping and must be awakened." So they cried aloud, and cut themselves, as was their custom, with knives and lances, until the blood gushed out on them. And when midday was past, they prophesied until the time of the offering of the evening sacrifice. But there was no voice; no one answered, no one paid attention.

A whole nation got to see with their own eyes what a big fat lie Baal was. "There was no voice; no one answered, no one paid attention." It is a precursor to revival for God to showcase the bankruptcy of the Woke religion.

Matthew Henry describes the humiliation of the prophets of Baal:

How importunate and noisy the prophets of Baal were in their applications to him. They got their sacrifices ready; and we may well imagine what a noise 450 men made, when they cried as one man, and with all their might, O Baal! hear us, O Baal! answer us; as it is in the margin: and this for some hours together, longer than Diana's worshippers made their cry, Great is Diana of the Ephesians (Acts 19:34). How senseless, how brutish, were they in their addresses to Baal!

(1.) Like fools, they leaped upon the altar, as if they would themselves become sacrifices with their bullock; or thus they expressed their great earnestness of mind. They leaped up and down or danced about the altar...they hoped, by their dancing, to please their deity, as Herodias' (daughter) did Herod, and so to obtain their request.

(2.) Like madmen they cut themselves in pieces with knives and lancets (v. 28) for vexation that they were not answered, or in a sort of prophetic fury, hoping to obtain the favor of their god by offering to him their own blood, when they could not obtain it with the blood of their bullock. God never required his worshippers thus to honor him; but the service of the devil, though in some instances it pleases and pampers the body, yet in other things it is really cruel to it, as in envy and drunkenness. It seems, this was the manner of the worshippers of Baal. God expressly forbade his worshipers to cut themselves (Deut. 14:1).[8]

Then the false prophets finally stopped. A lie bled to death. A nation watched to see what the prophet would do. It was his turn now.

It was one of the greatest demonstrations of supernatural power in history. But God needed a special prophet to oversee this astonishing event, just as America needs prophets today.

Tragically, we are saddled with a lot of self-proclaimed prophets. The church is enduring what I call the "God is about to" movement. They repeatedly tell us what God is about to do. And when their predictions do not come true, they distract the audience by declaring the next thing God is about to do. I sometimes think it would be stunning to see how many prophets and apostles would instantly vanish if Facebook ever shut down.

But Elijah was the man for this moment. Dead to his own purposes. Oblivious to personal safety. Totally focused and supremely confident. So confident that he lets the false prophets go first.

> Now Elijah said to the prophets of Baal, "Choose one bull for yourselves and prepare it first, for you are many; and call on the name of your god, but put no fire under it."
>
> —1 KINGS 18:25

Long before the fire fell, God had begun to dismantle Baal worship—first, by sending a drought. Baal was considered a god of rain and storm. So Israel was already wondering what the deal with Baal was.

By letting the false prophets go first, Elijah was letting everyone see that Baal was utter nonsense. Several hours of crying out to Baal with no answer would do the job.

Note: When God is healing a nation, He often lets the people gorge on their stupidity instead of blessing them with a miracle. He does it until no one is confused about the miserable failure of their false religion. On Mount Carmel, God was not just exposing Baal but draining the life out of him.

It was right for Elijah to make fun of their false god in verse 27. Preachers should be declaring from their pulpits how asinine the false religion of Wokeness is. Wokeness was supposed to be the god of economic justice, peace, and truth. They promised a drop in crime, national unity, and free stuff. Instead, every city under Woke rule is a festering cesspool of despair, addiction, violence, and murder.

Many of the modern-day Baal prophets overseeing these cities are fatally corrupted politicians. They are vile crooks who shun accountability and love to pose as civic heroes. Look back at what Baal's prophets did in verses 28–29, and then cry aloud to your god, you agents of Woke! Tell us again—how great will this be?

You had control of all the power and the money. Where did it go? Explain the nightmare. Explain how the answer to more crime was fewer police. Explain why your Wokeness made everything worse for our children, our schools, and our future. Explain why, instead of bringing unity, you have Americans at one another's throats. Bloviate again about how the rampant overdoses and spiking suicide rates are not your fault.

The verdict is in. The leftist, socialist makeover of America is a spectacular failure. It lies at America's feet as a pile of steaming, sputtering rubble. The same dead silence that settled over the prophets of Baal on Mount Carmel has settled over leftist America. The god of Woke can't answer. He is nowhere to be found because he does not exist.

TAKE STEPS LIKE ELIJAH'S

Now, at last, Elijah takes his turn in verses 30–35.

> Then Elijah said to all the people, "Come near to me." So, all the people came near to him. And he repaired the altar of the LORD that was broken down. And Elijah took twelve stones, according to the number of the tribes of the sons of Jacob, to whom the word of the LORD had come, saying, "Israel shall be your name." Then with the stones, he built an altar in the name of the LORD; and he made a trench around the altar large enough to hold two seahs of seed. And he put the wood in order, cut the bull in pieces, and laid it on the wood, and said, "Fill four waterpots with water, and pour it on the burnt sacrifice and on the wood." Then he said, "Do it a second time," and they did it a second time; and he said, "Do it a third time," and they did it a third time. So, the water ran all around the altar; and he also filled the trench with water.

"Come near to me," Elijah says. He wants a nation to crowd around and see the terrifying superiority of our God over all gods. He will take steps to create many degrees of separation between the living God and false gods. His every move is deliberate and by design.

First, Elijah rebuilds the torn-down altar of God. He dares not use the ready-made altar of Baal to sacrifice unto God. He is unmoved by the lateness of the day. He knows where God has ordained the fire to fall. Today's ministers should learn from his example.

The fire has not fallen because you used a contaminated altar. If you borrowed ideas and techniques of motivational speakers—if you blended in social-justice jargon to appear hip to your young audience—God will not answer by fire.

Never borrow worldly tricks or techniques to win the world to Christ. Never embellish the gospel or use clever language to sidestep God's rightful demands on people.

Above all, rebuilding God's altar today means returning to the Bible. Shame on those who tore down the Scriptures in favor of mystical experiences. And shame on preachers who have left it out of their sermons because "it offends the modern mind." Woe unto those who have cast doubt on the Bible's inerrancy.

Next, Elijah created another degree of separation between Jehovah and all other gods. He poured water on the altar—lots of water. He asked for more water. He ordered them to pour it out until it filled the trenches. Why did he do this? Priests of Baal were caught trying to slip fire into the wood on previous occasions. Elijah would remove all doubt. There would be no sleight of hand.

Elijah was declaring that there would be no tricks that day, only true power. That is what you are getting ready to do.

The Christian faith we declare stands apart from all other faiths on earth. It is the provable one. It is the eternal one. It is the power that prevails. Nothing else saves the soul from Satan and hell. Every religion of man fails bitterly to bring peace and joy. Presenting the truth of Christ simply and clearly is all we need to do. We carry the greatest power and best news humanity has ever heard.

It is time we start acting as if we know this is true. This is the right direction for us to take!

Next, Elijah uttered the prayer that changed history. Every word had design and power. If ever there were words that fit our situation, it is these words:

> And it came to pass, at the time of the offering of the evening sacrifice, that Elijah the prophet came near and said, "LORD God of Abraham, Isaac, and Israel, let it be known this day that You are God in Israel, and I am Your servant, and that I have done all these things at Your word. Hear me, O LORD, hear me, that this people may know that You are the LORD God, and that You have turned their hearts back to You again."
> —1 KINGS 18:36–37

Oh, that men and women of God would learn to pray—not for enjoyment or to bask in groovy feelings, not as rehab from a hard day. No, none of that. We need prayers that are said as if you were standing before God's mighty throne, beholding His inexpressible glory. Real prayer is a blend of holy fear at the awesomeness of the Father and holy boldness to ask for mighty things to happen.

Look at Elijah's title to address God: "LORD God of Abraham, Isaac, and Israel." He is speaking to God from the vantage point of history. By invoking the names of Abraham, Isaac, and Israel, Elijah reminds the people of the record of their awesome God and all His mighty acts.

The prophet dares not ask for fire until he has made two things clear:

1. whom he is talking to

2. why he is talking to Him

Hebrews 11:6 says, "But without faith it is impossible to please Him, for he who comes to God must believe that He is, and that He is a rewarder of those who diligently seek Him."

Why is Elijah talking to God? Because he knows what God wants. Jehovah wants to show them He is the God of Israel. Why is Elijah talking to God? Because God told him to. Elijah said, "I am Your servant, and...I have done all these things at Your word."

Then it happened!

> Then the fire of the LORD fell and consumed the burnt sacrifice, and the wood and the stones and the dust, and it licked up the water that was in the trench. Now when all the people saw it, they fell on their faces; and they said, "The LORD, He is God! The LORD, He is God!"
>
> —1 KINGS 18:38–39

Fire consuming the sacrifice would have been enough. But no! God wanted to make an emphatic statement. Nuclear fire vaporized the sacrifice on the altar, then the rocks, and then the water. How puny are all other gods! How surpassing is His power!

What does all this mean to you? It gives us the encouragement we need most right now. The grip of our wicked system seems just as unstoppable as Ahab and Jezebel. Evildoers are never brought to justice. The nation of America, founded on God, is being upended. The righteous are weary. We see nothing on the horizon to give us lasting hope for change.

What God did on Mount Carmel gives us the encouragement we need most right now. The fire did not just consume the meat, wood, stone, and water. It consumed an agenda—and not just any agenda but an intensely evil agenda. It was deeply entrenched. Its tentacles reached into every facet of Jewish life. It looked as if nothing could ever kill it. Then God answered by fire.

We need to see that! The same fire that evaporated seemingly unbreakable evil can destroy the Woke agenda in America—but only if we are headed in the right direction.

PART II:

FORCES THAT ARE RIPENING SOULS

Now we will see the backfire of the forces and factors that have been designed to destroy us.

Chapter 5

WOKE MISERY

THE ANGRY LEFT does not know they are building a massive backlash. I believe they are setting the stage to bring the greatest number of souls to Christianity in American history. Jesus made this amazing statement: "Do you think the work of harvesting will not begin until the summer ends four months from now? Look around you! Vast fields of human souls are ripening all around us, and are ready now for reaping" (John 4:35, TLB).

Human souls ripening? What makes a human soul ripen? We know that crops in fields and fruit in orchards ripen by tilling, feeding, pruning, watering, and sunlight. But human souls ripen in misery. God haters have tilled the soil and added the ingredients necessary to ripen vast fields of souls.

The Woke movement's biggest mistake was that they made everyone miserable. They created the kind of misery that leads to conversions. Now every drop of their emotional, intellectual, and spiritual madness seems to be backfiring on them. In short, people are sick to death of their extremes.

Wokeness drained the color, vitality, and enjoyment out of American life. The Woke crowd made everything offensive, suspicious, sinister, cruel, and even frightening. Because of them, millions are now groping in deep darkness and despair.

We are a nation in agony and pain. That ripens souls! C. S. Lewis wrote this: "Pain insists upon being attended to. God whispers to us in our pleasures, speaks in our conscience, but shouts in our pain: it is His megaphone to rouse a deaf world."[1]

In Matthew 9, Jesus gives us the connection between misery and souls becoming ripe for the gospel.

> When He saw the throngs, He was moved with pity and sympathy for them, because they were bewildered (harassed and distressed and dejected and helpless), like sheep without a shepherd. Then He said to His disciples, The harvest is indeed plentiful, but the laborers are few. So pray to the Lord of the harvest to force out and thrust laborers into His harvest.
> —Matthew 9:36–38, ampc

Jesus calls them sheep without a shepherd. There is no animal more pitiful than a sheep abandoned in the wild. They are the epitome of helplessness, confusion, and terror. This is the perfect analogy for the people living in Jesus' day. They had been invaded by Romans, betrayed by their government, and crushed under the rules and regulations of hypocritical Pharisees.

But then something happened. They ran to hear a voice crying in the wilderness. John the Baptist created such a massive and intense stampede the people could not help themselves. And he did it despite the harsh message of repentance. All Judea went out to be baptized in the wilderness.

They asked Jesus to explain this phenomenon, and He replied, "And from the days of John the Baptist until now the kingdom of heaven suffers violence, and the violent take it by force" (Matt. 11:12).

Notice two words: *violence* and *force*. It was not just a massive response; it was a fierce response. It was deep and wide. Two extremes collided. The total despair of the people crashed head-on into an open revelation of God.

Jesus is the only One who can fulfill the deepest desires of the human heart. Pascal believed every heart has a God-shaped vacuum that cannot be satisfied by any created thing but only by God the Creator. He wrote:

What else does this craving, and this helplessness, proclaim but that there was once in man a true happiness, of which all that now remains is the empty print and trace? This he tries in vain to fill with everything around him, seeking in things that are not there the help he cannot find in those that are, though none can help, since this infinite abyss can be filled only with an infinite and immutable object; in other words by God himself.[2]

But the evil that men do can intensify that vacuum.

I want to cite a verse that seems unrelated. Haggai 2:7 (KJV) says, "I will shake all nations, and the desire of all nations shall come."

This unique prophecy has a double meaning. First, it refers to the wealth of all the nations flowing into the temple in Jerusalem. The rest of the verse promises that God will fill the rebuilt temple with His glory.

Believers have traditionally seen this as a promise of Christ's coming because Jesus referred to His body in John 2:20–21 as "this temple."

Jesus is the ultimate "desire of all nations" and is only reached because of the vacuum Pascal described. And if they hear His voice, they will come running.

What does a sheep lost in the wild yearn for? More than food, more than warmth, it yearns for the shepherd. That is what is happening to Americans.

Leftists believe they are improving us! Instead, they are creating deep yearnings that transcend food, money, or even security. The yearnings are maturing into a widespread cry to God.

Jesus is the deepest desire of mankind—even when they don't know it. The cold, brutal emptiness of the atheistic agenda intensifies that desire.

I see this every night in the tent. Sitting before me are the trophies of modern perversion: tattoos, spiked hair, boys in dresses, and young girls dressed as men. They are addicted and angry to the point of suicide.

Then they hear His voice. The tears burst forth, and they do not care who sees. They run to Christ. And God rushes to meet them.

The secular progressives plan to erase Christianity in America. They are certain they can replace faith and the Bible with a purely secular society. Their playbook is intricate and patient. They have forged their manifesto, and they've gone to work.

Their operatives fanned out into every feasible institution of American life. Many of them started at the bottom—community organizers in poor neighborhoods. Soon they controlled teachers' unions, newspapers, radio, television, universities, Hollywood, churches, social media, and finally the White House. Their goal is a socialist utopia.

Socialism is an entry-level drug that leads to communism. Even Lenin said, "The goal of socialism is communism."[3] Socialism is the hippie stage of Marxism. It's the daisy you don't notice is sticking out of the end of a rifle.

Low-level socialists have an idealistic view of human nature. They think people are naturally inclined toward sociable cooperation. Ironically, human nature is the reason people try socialism, and human nature is why socialism fails every time it is tried.

To paraphrase the old saying, if you aren't a socialist at twenty-five, you don't have a heart; if you are still a socialist at thirty-five, you don't have a brain.

Do you want to kill hope and incentive? The best way I know is to rip the hard-earned money from someone's hand and give it to another who refuses to work. Those who make an effort will see no point in continuing to try. And when some get paid to do nothing, everyone will want to get paid to do nothing.

We already see it. Expanded unemployment benefits during the pandemic created a massive worker shortage.[4] Many people simply did not return to work when it was over. Perhaps they thought the government would finance a permanent vacation. Restaurants shortened their hours, and many closed. Airline delays became massive, and the quality of our service industry, manufacturing, and products tanked. Our economy entered a recession.

And all of it groomed us for a very different way of life. Look at our current condition through the lens of this quote from Ayn Rand:

> When you see that in order to produce, you need to obtain permission from men who produce nothing—when you see that money is flowing to those who deal, not in goods, but in favors—when you see that men get richer by graft and by pull than by work, and your laws don't protect you against them, but protect them against you—when you see corruption being rewarded and honesty becoming a self-sacrifice—you may know that your society is doomed.[5]

This quote takes us to the most hideous fact about communism: the dark money. In the leftist pyramid I see three levels of power. The bottom level is the idealist youth, who are highly impressionable. The second level is the true believer activists, who seem to be running the show. These are the secular progressive leaders. I believe they know that what they are doing does not work. They are lying to their underlings.

Then there is a third level: the dark money. Dark-money people have existed throughout modern history. They lurk in shadowy corners and prey on the masses. They use their wealth to buy and manipulate nations and crush freedom.

While secular progressive leaders were busy trying to fool our youth, the dark money fooled them.

Dark money reached its zenith around the year 2020. That is when they were ready to test their control mechanism under the perfect camouflage of a virus. They discovered that they could shut down churches and cities, kill hundreds of thousands of small businesses, and dramatically increase the size and power of government.

What is shocking is that the American church took the bait faster than most other institutions. Faulty theology was mostly to blame. It is interesting how the devil works. When he wants free rein in a sector of society, he will seduce the church into believing that sector is off-limits to Christians. Right now, that sector is politics.

The devil told preachers that God wanted them out of politics. They believed him. Then the devil went to work unimpeded and unchallenged to write wicked laws.

Even with glaring examples of politicians doing evil at this hour, preachers remain silent. Worse, they are putting the label of "Christian nationalist" on anyone who speaks out against them—as if to be Christian and love America is a slur.

Christians being involved in politics is not new. Almost fifty years ago Francis Schaeffer said everything that so-called Christian nationalists are saying now in his plea for American Christians to wake up politically. John Fea, professor of American history at Messiah College in Pennsylvania, said:

> From his chalet in the Swiss Alps, Schaeffer influenced an entire generation of evangelical culture warriors. In his popular book and later film series, *How Shall We Then Live: The Rise and Decline of Western Thought and Culture* (1976), he convinced evangelicals that secularism was born out of Renaissance humanism and, if allowed to grow in influence, it would inevitably lead to the collapse of Western civilisation. The survival of Christendom was at stake and the lives of babies in the womb were at risk. The U.S. had lost its moral center. Schaeffer wrote and spoke with a sense of urgency that moved evangelical Christians to political action.[6]

This is far more important than it seems. First, it proves that political action is not new to the church—burying your head in the sand is what is new. Next, it proves that Christian college students—who were Schaeffer's primary audience—were some of the earliest Christian conservatives. And finally, this occurred during the Jesus movement, which directly connects today's Christian political activism and that great youth revival.

But the most important fact is that it proves the church has seen God challenge and overcome the Left before. And God did it through the youth! I believe He is about to do it again.

First Samuel 3:1 tells us, "Now the boy Samuel ministered to the LORD before Eli. And the word of the LORD was rare in those days; there was no widespread revelation." Neither Eli nor the Israelites realized revelation from God was indeed about to touch them again—and it would come through a little boy.

Think of a hurricane. The air pressure drops dramatically over the ocean. Nature abhors a vacuum and creates violent winds to fill that vacuum. The same applies to cultural vacuums.

Remove decency, ban God, pervert justice, enforce oppressive laws, and then ban all opposing views. This doesn't create a utopia. It creates a vacuum. You create a voracious appetite for any good thing that you have made scarce. It creates the very thing that will undo the brave new world they are trying to create.

Jeremiah 2:11 asks, "Has a nation changed its gods?" The prophet is accusing Israel of a disastrous mistake: exchanging Jehovah for an idol. America has also changed its gods. Wokeism and leftist socialism are our new religions. They have created a massive void in the soul of America. Our mistake is so deep we cannot find the bottom.

Woke domination has turned major American cities into cesspools of despair, corruption, and mass murder. The leftist gender revolution has destroyed innocence. Education has declared war on parents and childhood itself. The Woke agenda swept in like a plague of locusts and consumed everything.

But the devastating part for the Left is that Americans are realizing exactly whom to blame. They know who destroyed the beauty and innocence of America. They already know who is responsible for inflation, who wrote the depraved government policies, who sexualized their children without their permission, who lied to them, who released murderers into their neighborhoods, and who set their future on fire.

The same utter misery Jesus saw in the first century He sees in our nation today. That means if the same wind of the Holy Spirit blows over our nation, it will produce the same widespread and intense invasion into the kingdom.

Many generations of believers have witnessed revivals. They knew what it meant to see a sudden and vast influx of people. Now it is our turn, which is both good and bad news.

It is good because it can redeem our nation from the abyss. It is good because churches will double in size overnight.

It is bad because we are ill-prepared. Our church culture is almost anti–soul winning. It is bad because we have an entire generation of self-absorbed individuals who do not know how to serve. They were preached into that condition.

The stampede, while wonderful, is equally terrifying. Here's the thing: harvests are never calm or easy. But a bumper crop is another thing altogether. The farmer faces the sudden reality that "all the crops in the field are ripening at the same time! I need to hire all the help I can find, and fast!" Awakenings are like that.

Not only that, but we are used to church growth in a hostile environment. That means the only growth we see is slow and comes by getting members from other churches. Our mindset will jeopardize the harvest.

Harvests wait for no one. Vast fields are ripening. Ready or not, here they come.

I am already seeing it. In our recent crusade, we had fifteen hundred volunteers. Some were concerned that we had too many workers. They worried they would be standing around the tent with little to do. Many of them were shocked when that same night more than fifteen hundred souls poured into the front of the tent. We needed every available worker—and then some!

The other challenge we will face is their zeal. The converts will be on fire. They will not need the life-support systems we have created for the lukewarm. The sermons that the fashionable Christian calls outdated and fanatical will thrill new converts. They will keep praying when everyone wants to stop. They will witness with fearless joy.

The good news is that it's our turn now. The bad news is that we are not ready. But the best news is that we *will* be ready. God is taking you aside to train you. He is not preparing you for a normal, predictable life.

You stand where previous vessels of God stood. They felt the same inadequacy you feel. You have no clue how God will do it. Neither did they. It is your turn to be forged in the fire and come forth as gold. It is your turn to know Him in the power of His resurrection. It is your turn to turn the tide, exploit the enemy, and glorify God in an impossible situation.

Of course, there will be critics of everything I am saying here. They will use a microscope to find fault. They will tell you that I am oversimplifying the current situation. Others will say we must revert to practical ways and be content with "realistic" results. Still others will tell you that such a massive influx is impossible and that I should not be awakening a false hope.

What if I'm wrong? I know I am not. But for the sake of argument, let's say that you pray, study, prepare, believe, and set yourself for this turning to God, and what comes is not what we expect. At the very least you are a sharpened edge, with a clear heart and mind to be ready for anything. But I believe there is no way for you—in this situation—to be all dressed up with nowhere to go.

On the other hand, what if I'm right? I know that I am. What if you don't prepare, train, and believe? Imagine something this glorious coming and you miss it because you did not prepare or train, and you are sidelined and distracted. That would be the absolute worst thing.

I am rejoicing because I know what God is doing. And it is wonderful beyond words. I repeat a verse I quoted before: "I want to report to you, friends, that my imprisonment here has had the opposite of its intended effect. Instead of being squelched, the Message has actually prospered" (Phil. 1:12, MSG).

"The opposite of its intended effect." They meant to chase people away from Christ. Instead, they are causing a stampede toward Him. They wanted to legislate immorality; instead, a heartsick nation will seek the soul-cleansing power of the blood of Jesus. They intended to censor the things of God. But soon the things of God will be everywhere!

Chapter 6

IT'S ALL ABOUT THE CHILDREN

THE LOCAL YMCA in Port Townsend, Washington, permanently banned eighty-year-old Julie Jaman from the pool. Her crime? Daring to object to a trans woman (a man) using the women's locker room.

In Jaman's words, "I saw a man in a woman's bathing suit watching maybe four or five little girls pulling down their suits in order to use the toilet....I asked if he had a penis and he said it was none of my business. I told that man to 'get out right now.'"

Here's the rest of the story:

> For exercising what would have been universally praised not long ago as guts and common sense—confronting a man trespassing in a women's locker room to watch little girls undress—Jaman was accused of "being discriminatory" by the YMCA manager, threatened with the police, and ordered to leave. A member of the YMCA for 35 years, she was subsequently banned from the pool permanently.
>
> Jaman's ordeal wasn't over, though. On Monday, Jaman and others gathered to speak out about the local YMCA's dangerous policy of allowing men into the women's locker room. As Jaman was speaking, a mob of Antifa militants, including burly, tattooed men, converged on the rally, screaming, "Trans women are women," in an attempt to intimidate and drown her out. They ripped down the suffragette flags on display behind Jaman, who was visibly shaken and asked, "Are we going to get beat up here?" and asked supporters in the crowd to call the police.

Eventually, the Antifa mob surrounded Jaman, whose supporters, most of them middle-aged and elderly women, had to form a protective circle around her. Some women were thrown to the ground. Others had their shoes ripped off. Just as black-shirted Antifa men were beginning to tussle with Jaman's supporters, the police showed up.

It wasn't enough, though, simply to terrorize and physically assault women exercising their First Amendment rights. The mayor of Port Townsend, a self-described "pervert and deviant" named David J. Faber, praised the mob that went after Jaman and her supporters, calling it an "incredible night" that was "beautiful" and falsely claiming that "Trans and cis-allies alike spoke love & support."

As copious video evidence posted on Twitter shows, they did no such thing. They engaged in the thuggish intolerance, simmering violence, and blind rage characteristic of the far left—and then they reveled in it, with the likes of Faber praising the mob for their brutality toward an 80-year-old woman who dared to speak up.[1]

Without a doubt, the most explosive issues with the transgender movement concern children and teens.

On July 6, 2022, The Daily Wire carried this headline: "Award-Winning Drag Queen, LGBTQ Youth Adviser Charged With 25 Counts of Child Pornography."[2]

> Williams, twenty-six, of Chambersburg, is charged with twenty-five counts of child pornography for at least forty-nine photos and twenty-five videos of naked, prepubescent boys that the Pennsylvania Attorney General's Office said he downloaded between May and December 2020. The sexually-explicit content showed genitalia and boys performing sex acts on one another, according to an affidavit of probable cause filed Thursday.[3]

Even this infamy will be fact-checked into oblivion. And anyone who calls this out will face the wrath of Wokesters. Transgender ideology has infiltrated public schools, hospitals, and higher education. Its adherents will not leave you alone.

By the way, if you think overturning *Roe v. Wade* has put Planned Parenthood out of business, think again. They have "transitioned" their business model to gender bending. Even in states that have banned abortions, not one Planned Parenthood location has closed. They remain open under the guise of "gender-affirming care"—a freshly minted term for "addressing gender dysphoria, especially in children and young teens, through surgery, puberty blockers, and cross-sex hormones. It is better thought of as profitable, appearance-altering, experimental protocols, with very little oversight or regulation, though sometimes it is funded by taxpayers."[4]

THE WAR ON PARENTS

How can this possibly be happening in America? It is happening because the Woke mob and their leftist sympathizers have declared war on children to appease their base. But they have also declared war on parents.

And ironically, the vanguard of the war on parents is teachers! A blog post on the American Federation of Teachers' Share My Lesson website claims there are parents who "will make it their job to undermine" teachers. The post was reported on Fox News by Kelsey Koberg on August 12, 2022.[5]

But the war on parents doesn't stop there. Classrooms around the country are intentionally circumventing the authority of parents in an increasingly alarming fashion.

On August 10, 2022, Fox News carried this headline: "AFT union promotes method for teachers to help kids change their pronouns without parents knowing."

> The American Federation of Teachers promoted the use of a pronoun card which included a question of whether the

student wanted their parents to know about their pronouns, Fox News Digital has learned.

The AFT's "Share My Lesson" website promoted using the cards in an "all" grade levels section, such as middle school. "Something as simple as a Student Introduction Card could make a student feel seen and affirmed," the lesson, by the AFT's Vision and Mission of the Identity Affirming Classroom Team, said.[6]

On August 10, 2022, The Federalist online magazine reported that a male teacher asked an eleven-year-old girl to sleep in the boys' cabin without telling her parents. It began with therapy at school.

So, for two and a half months, Jennifer's daughter was meeting with a school therapist once a week who was treating her as a boy, using male pronouns and a made-up name. When Jennifer would ask how the sessions were going, the therapist acted as though nothing big had come up.

Then in February 2020, right before COVID-19 hit, Jennifer received a phone call from the school therapist with a two-fold purpose: to request that she and her husband come to the school in three days for a meeting where the therapist would assist their daughter in officially coming out to them as a boy, and to obtain parental permission to allow her daughter to stay overnight in the [boys'] cabin for an upcoming school trip.

Jennifer and her husband canceled the appointment.

At that point, Jennifer and her husband decided to take more drastic measures. They were skeptical that their eleven-year-old daughter was transgender and believed the school and the therapist were actually leading her to identify as a boy. So, they revoked their consent for their daughter to see the school therapist, took away her access to online devices, and soon, unenrolled her from public school altogether.[7]

This was when the delusion wore off. The little girl was trying to fit in, and the school leaders were not just affirming and encouraging gender delusion; they were teaching kids to deny their own perceptions. Once the girl was removed, all her confusion lifted.

THE WAR ON CHILDREN

Now we get to the part I want to hammer home. Another trend—the war on children—will drive souls to Jesus in America. Jennifer's experience shattered her faith in people she had previously looked up to.

> Jennifer feels betrayed by educators, therapists, doctors, and liberal politicians whom she spent a lifetime supporting. That list includes President Joe Biden, who told parents in March that affirming their child's transgender identity is "one of the most powerful things you can do to keep them safe and healthy."

For politicians to say these things is appalling, in my opinion. In the past, most parents would have taken the wait-and-see approach, and the vast majority of kids expressing any type of gender curiosity or confusion would not end up opting to be medically or socially transitioned. But today parents are being told the only acceptable response is affirmation. Jennifer's story proves there can be different outcomes when a child's uncomfortable feelings about gender are not affirmed. "They might desist," she said. "Isn't that preferable to a lifetime of harmful medical procedures?"[8]

But this chapter is not designed simply to evoke outrage. There is a factor here. The Left had America sealed up. The Woke agenda was flying high, with no end in sight. Then they made the mistake of targeting children.

Think of it. How many other Jennifers are out there? They live in deep blue states. They have supported liberal policies most of their lives. But liberalism was always happening to other people. And it was believable until Woke walked in. Then everything turned dark and vicious.

Many strong leftists have defected and are now conservatives because of vaccine mandates. In June 2022 it was reported that more than one million voters across forty-three states had switched parties to the GOP over the previous year.[9] Vaccine mandates were listed as one of the reasons—not to mention CRT and the endless list of absurdities that clings to Wokeness. But nothing compares to our children. When they come calling for your child, everything changes.

In times past they had always tried to keep children out of their pernicious ways. They could hold on to their mesmerized following. Then they had drag queens start reading stories to little ones and afterward rolling around on the floor with them.[10] They had children parading on catwalks with sexualized adult models.[11] Now they are lowering the age limits for children to take hormone blockers and get gender-transfer surgeries too sickening to describe here.[12]

It was always about the children. Our sin looks harmless until we do it in front of them. And the fact that we want to do it in front of them reveals the depth of our depravity.

At some point you must believe your eyes. You know what male and female are. Only a parent overtaken by debauchery can celebrate their four-year-old girl for saying she wants to be a boy.

MY WARNING FOR THE WOKE—AND THE AWAKENED

Woke leaders want parents to subject their children to more and more that they cannot go along with—things that are simply too malicious to do to someone you love more than your own life.

So, Mr. and Ms. Woke, I have a warning for you: you will lose parents by the millions—all because of the horrified look in the eyes of a child. All because you know in your heart the evil that hides behind the rights, platitudes, and inclusiveness.

Your movement is not noble. It's no advancement of justice or truth; it's the dregs of society rising from intellectual manholes. You can't hide the stench. You can't hide your predatory eyes. There is nothing decent about what you want to put on children. Your uncleanness is deeper than words. Even your light is darkness.

So go ahead and keep pushing the limits. Keep calling degradation progress. Your philosophy is dead, and the stench of the corpse is spreading. Masses of parents have seen your snake oil and the vile and putrid sores under your mask. They are taking their little ones by the hand and saying, "Come on, let's go home."

Soldier of Christ, hear me out. Now that parents see what Wokeness does to children, they will yearn for the truth. They will want to be right with God just to protect their children.

Malachi 4:5–6 says, "Behold, I will send you Elijah the prophet before the coming of the great and dreadful day of the LORD. And he will turn the hearts of the fathers to the children, and the hearts of the children to their fathers, lest I come and strike the earth with a curse."

Because of children, hearts are turning. Because of children, tears will return to eyes long dry and hearts hardened from sin. A thirst for innocence and sudden nausea over wickedness will soon send them to be saved, all because of their children.

An hour such as America has never seen will come because we finally realize they do not want to help our children; they want to disfigure them. Parents will no longer want to take children to events that sexualize them and steal their childhood. Parents will no longer let them become trophies of Satan's dark and evil plan.

Where, then, will they take them? Matthew 19:14: "But Jesus said, 'Let the little children come to Me, and do not forbid them; for of such is the kingdom of heaven.'"

Chapter 7

THE COMING BACKFIRE BY YOUTH

A GENERATION OF YOUNG students decides to unleash its fury on American cities. In one city, they march down streets setting homes, businesses, and even police cars on fire. The city is engulfed in smoke and flames. Every business has shattered windows. It takes thousands of county sheriffs and national guardsmen several days to restore order.

Am I describing Minneapolis and the BLM riots after George Floyd? No, these were the anti-war riots in Berkeley, California, during the mid-1970s. I know because I was there.

Resurrection City was the name of our outreach to the University of California at Berkeley. It consisted of a fourplex apartment building with a small chapel in the back. Because we were Christian, I was sure the demonstrators would want to burn us out.

I sent our workers home to their parents. The rioters loved to attack at night. I heard them coming and ran out front. I had no idea what to do or how to protect our center. I ended up leaning on the hood of my car with a garden hose running, thinking, "What good is a garden hose against this horde?"

The mob came to a stop in front of our building. I braced for the worst. And what happened next would change my life forever. While the rioters were screaming to burn down our center, their leader got on a megaphone and said, "These are good people. Do not burn their building. Pass over this one!"

Why did he say "pass over"? Of all the words he could have chosen, he chose the words that would echo in my heart for years afterward. I tell people all the time that this was our personal Passover.

That single sign from God told me we were right where we belonged. I called my team back, and we possessed the land. Starting with a handful of students, we invaded the campus. Soon we were ninety people strong. Then it was two hundred. Then five hundred. We never stopped growing for ten years. Our rallies drew thousands, and the riots decreased until they became minor disturbances.

You may think you know why I told you that story. Surely, I told you so you could rejoice with me over a miraculous testimony. Right? No. I told you about this to give you an important insight. But that insight is meaningless if you don't first appreciate what I am about to tell you.

On campuses across America, vast armies of students were committed to the Marxist revolution. There was no inkling of desire for Christianity on university campuses. The April 8, 1966, cover of *Time* magazine asked, "Is God Dead?"

A blanket of deception settled on young people. It seemed that nothing could ever reach them. Then it happened. The Holy Spirit fell on California. Overnight, we had a moral revolution on our hands.

Young people with long hair and bare feet flooded into churches. In Southern California many beaches witnessed the unimaginable. Thousands came to be baptized in the ocean on the same sands where drugs and free love had reigned supreme.

Christian festivals sprang up in many parts of our nation. Crowds for these events ranged from ten thousand to seventy-two thousand. Contemporary Christian music became a permanent part of American culture.

Signs had warned that it was coming, but the idea was so fantastic that experts missed them. Church denominations were caught totally by surprise. Christian leaders did not recognize the hour of their visitation. Some even fought against the very thing they had fervently prayed for. How foolish that seems now.

But before we judge the church too harshly for being utterly oblivious, we need to realize something. In many respects the generation of the '60s and '70s was in worse shape than kids today. In addition to the rise of the psychedelic-drug culture led by Timothy Leary and others, the anger and tension of this generation had reached a boiling point. I look at today's Antifa thugs, and they remind me of something out of a Renaissance fair, compared with the Left-wing domestic terrorists of the 1970s.

The Weather Underground, a far-Left militant organization led by Bill Ayers, conducted a campaign of bombing public buildings (including police stations, the Capitol, and the Pentagon) during the 1960s and 1970s in response to US involvement in the Vietnam War.

The anti-war protests of that era were gigantic and could shut down entire universities. They could hold the biggest cities' downtown areas hostage with their demonstrations.

The bottom line is that churches were dead, and in their mind the youth were too far gone to evangelize. Instead, preachers and parents focused on keeping church kids away from evil influences. Consequently, the church had no strategy for dealing with a shocking act of God on a youth culture they thought was beyond saving.

It is easy to see why they missed their great awakening. Thank God they finally realized that these "Jesus freaks" were an astonishing blessing.

It would be equally stupid for us to ignore the signs of another youth awakening. We must learn from past mistakes. We must see through the images of their perversions. We must not be put off by their extremes. What they say and do looks for all the world to be impervious to God. But they may be more susceptible than we imagined.

Remember, youths feel the brunt whenever there is a great social change. It falls on them. They glom on to a new idea—especially if that idea is popular among their peers—and run with it. They take it to extremes.

The tragedy for this generation is that the ideas they run with are dark and full of despair. They are taught to be ashamed and suspicious of themselves. It began as an issue of race and things like white privilege, but now it is greatly expanded to be a nihilistic self-hatred.

They are told they are a disease on an innocent planet and dare not reproduce. They must pay for the sins of previous generations—sins they have nothing to do with.

No one comes out of critical race theory a winner. It victimizes everyone and offers no solution for the disaster of man that they claim to have discovered. Black children come out with a mindset of unending victimhood, and white children come out feeling like unredeemable villains.

This feel-bad-about-yourself movement now saturates education. On a television show, eminent clinical psychologist Jordan Peterson was asked this question: "Incoming freshmen next year, University of Toronto, Stanford University, eighteen-year-old kids coming into this. We've been through three years of Covid—I won't rehearse it all. One sentence. What would you say to them as they begin university at the age of eighteen or nineteen? What's the restorative? The redemptive sentence? What should they do?"

Peterson's answer was this: "Don't be thinking your ambition is corrupt. Because that's part of the message. Human beings were a cancer on the planet, which means we are heading for an environmental apocalypse. The entire historical structure is nothing but atrocity, etc., etc. Anyone with any ethical claim whatsoever is just going to pull back. You don't want to manifest any ambition, support the patriarchal structure, exploit the environment. You've got to crush yourself down. You shouldn't even have any children."

And then he displayed genuine outrage for what Wokeism is doing to the next generation. "You're going to demoralize young people to be ethical? That's your theory? You should go home and think about that, for like, a year. I'm passionate about this because you have no idea how many people that's killing. You have no idea. I see people every day, all over the world. They are so demoralized. Especially young people. Especially young people with a conscience. Because they have been told since they were little that there is nothing to them but corruption and power."[1]

The good news is that this lie is not sustainable. It is wearing thin on a generation growing skeptical of the constant drip of despair.

In an August 21, 2022, article in *The Epoch Times,* young podcasters with a booming audience—former leftists who were now conservative—unapologetically questioned the Left's pervading narratives.

The article stated:

> "We are seeing young people grow up with the mindset that they need to reduce themselves down to race, gender, and their sexuality," Amala Ekpunobi, host of the podcast "Unapologetic," told The Epoch Times. "Those three very superficial identities have become so pivotal in how people introduce themselves and whether they are viewed as victims or champions. The more we go down the path of this false narrative, the more we are oppressing them and entertaining a culture of victimhood that is sheerly unsustainable." …
>
> "I think the most hard-hitting issue for me was race," Ekpunobi said. "I grew up in a white family. I'm biracial. My father is from Nigeria, and my mother, who works with the political Left, is white."
>
> As a child, Ekpunobi aligned herself with her mother's views, becoming an activist throughout middle and high school, she said, until she became a paid activist after graduating.
>
> It was then when she began observing hypocrisy within the organization, she said.
>
> "I heard a lot of racism toward white people behind the walls of this organization," she said.

Ekpunobi confronted the organizers about it, asking how they could claim to be the tolerant, anti-racists when they themselves were making racist comments.

"I was told that I was simply unaware of how oppressed I was and that it wasn't their fault that I wasn't angry, but that I should be, because of how I was treated in this country," Ekpunobi said...."I had always grown up with the idea that white people carry these inherent biases and that they were a part of a structure of oppression that was working against me, whether they knew it or not," Ekpunobi said. "So, it was really difficult there toward the end to justify having those opinions, then going home to a family who cared for me."

"The [woke] worldview is limiting and distorted," Ekpunobi explained, "and it's robbing young people of their opportunity to have fulfillment in life and a vision of a future in which they can choose from a wide range of vocations, unlimited by their race and gender."...

Like Ekpunobi, ex-Democrat Judith Rose's shift from woke to awake took place after an investigation into her own pro-gramming and its sources....Rose had begun to see an agenda behind every message broadcasted from legacy media outlets, she said, and those messages appeared to be making people sick....

"Even after getting off social media, I could see that I was being radicalized through fake media news that crafts these emotional, opinion-based headlines," she said. "That's what was happening to me: I had been flipping through these head-lines and basing my opinions on those."

What passes for so many as education and news, Rose said, is in fact propaganda designed as a component of manipula-tive social experiments with the endgame of dehumanizing and controlling people.

"People are being introduced to ideas that they normally would have no reason to look at, and then there's this mecha-nism that's adopting new terms and changing language," she said. "It's very Orwellian, and it's very unsettling."

Rose also observed what she believed to be not only a mental illness but a spiritual sickness behind the "extreme emotional reactions" in herself and others when their ideologies conflicted with opposing views.

"I had to sit down and acknowledge that I was overly angry and didn't understand why," Rose said. "I had to do a lot of meditating, and reaching out to God and say, 'Hey, I don't understand this world, can you help me?'"[2]

Look at how her despair drove her to reach out to God. The conflict she describes is not just happening to her. I believe it is taking place on a massive scale. That is what I am trying to tell you! The evil leaders of Woke philosophy are setting the stage for the next wave of conversions.

These two young women represent a segment of the youth culture. But there are many other segments and many other ways that youth are going from Woke to awake. And those ready for harvesting are all ripening at the same time.

I told you that the misery of Woke is ripening vast fields of human souls. That is the first trend. Then I showed you the trend of parents who love their children. But this youth trend is even more explosive than the other two. Why?

Christianity has always been a youth movement. Many of the great American revivals have started on campuses. The Jesus movement was powerful and widespread for one reason: it was young people.

When our youth get hold of the gospel, it will create a holy peer pressure. Satan will see their youthful energy combined with the fire of the Holy Spirit as a lethal combination.

I want you to conclude that even though our youth generation is in the throes of great deception and looks utterly lost and disinterested in Christ, there is a great spiritual upheaval within them. That upheaval will be seized by Christ. He will draw them to Himself in vast numbers.

We are about to witness the fulfillment of a prophecy given many centuries ago by the prophet Joel and quoted by Peter on the day of Pentecost.

> And it shall come to pass in the last days, says God, that I will pour out of My Spirit on all flesh; your sons and your daughters shall prophesy, your young men shall see visions, your old men shall dream dreams. And on My menservants and on My maidservants I will pour out My Spirit in those days; and they shall prophesy. I will show wonders in heaven above and signs in the earth beneath: blood and fire and vapor of smoke. The sun shall be turned into darkness, and the moon into blood, before the coming of the great and awesome day of the LORD. And it shall come to pass that whoever calls on the name of the LORD shall be saved.
>
> —ACTS 2:17–21

Chapter 8

SUPERNATURAL MISFITS: GOD'S SECRET WEAPON

ALL THE TRENDS we have examined so far are outside the church. But the most explosive trend is inside the church.

We are talking about a group of people. They are the most overlooked and underestimated force in the church. They are neither rebels nor extremists. But they just do not fit in "regular" religion.

David Wilkerson gave the best description of them. He said, "God-hungry people are saying among themselves, 'This is not it. There is something more. The bigness and the sensationalism of it all has left us empty and dry. We want more. More than entertainment. More than big, showy buildings. More than a shallow celebrity gospel. We want deeper values. We want to see Jesus. We want spotless robes of righteousness. We want to go back to doing things in total dependence on God."[1]

Many of these people were chased out of once fiery, Spirit-filled churches. They saw their church become obsessed with impressing outsiders. They no longer feel the presence of the Holy Spirit in the worship services.

What are their chief complaints? They see the world system operating in the church. They can't stomach the fact that prayer and anointed preaching have been replaced. The house of God is now a glitzy entertainment center.

They are deeply hurt that their church punishes them for wanting a move of God but at the same time caters to lukewarm members.

What is the urgency that drives this group of people? They see America on the verge of destruction. They believe we have no time to play games.

They are done with egocentric preachers with grandiose, expensive, and carnal visions that have nothing to do with soul winning or revival. They accuse these preachers of being distracted and even derailed from their first love.

These "God-hungry people," as David Wilkerson calls them, are abandoning attraction churches in record numbers. Something revolutionary is happening inside them.

But are they right with God? Is their passion selfish? What could be wrong with making the church alluring to outsiders? The rising core has clear responses to these questions.

Don't get me wrong, these misfits believe in big churches. They simply affirm that the best big church is a Holy Spirit–driven church. Only by the Holy Spirit can we get the quantity and quality He desires to see in church members.

The marketing approach to outreach leaves out the key ingredient: repentance. Repentance unlocks the new creation. Repentance is the active ingredient in a victorious Christian life.

But I want to identify their greatest frustration: seeing the flood of evil the devil is pouring out into the world while passive Christians are watching all this evil happen. They are frustrated that the church does not realize the role God wants them to play in His warfare against Satan.

This is the worst possible time for Christians to ignore the things going on in our country. It is not the time for God's people to be enthralled by unimportant issues and ignore crucial matters.

So here is what is going on. While the Holy Spirit is brooding over a sin-sick nation and causing a hunger for salvation, He is also working within the church to create the army that will bring in the massive harvest.

That makes this rising core extremely special. They are an answer to prayer. Remember what Jesus said to His disciples in

Matthew 9:37–38: "The harvest truly is plentiful, but the laborers are few. Therefore, pray the Lord of the harvest to send out laborers into His harvest."

They are neither what the church expected nor wanted, but they are an answer to prayer.

The church is not ready for the harvest. Imagine the shame and embarrassment when a generation comes knocking on the door of the church, exclaiming, "Please give us Jesus! We do not need big screens, skinny jeans, or fog machines! We want the Bible. We want the fire of the Holy Spirit."

We need to wake up! Explosions are going on all around us. Parents are at the end of their ropes. Youth are coming unraveled on a massive scale. A volcano is rumbling in the hearts of a huge group of Christians. Society itself is reaching critical mass. We need to discern what all this means.

Jesus said in Matthew 16:2–3, "When it is evening you say, 'It will be fair weather, for the sky is red'; and in the morning, 'It will be foul weather today, for the sky is red and threatening.' Hypocrites! You know how to discern the face of the sky, but you cannot discern the signs of the times."

We must discern the signs! All these hindrances and obstacles are hiding a growing phenomenon. The unseen hand of God is putting the pieces together.

No one can build an army the way God can. No one can gather them when there seems to be nothing to gather. Even Elijah felt so alone that he doubted God's power to reserve a core. God said, "Yet I have reserved seven thousand in Israel, all whose knees have not bowed to Baal, and every mouth that has not kissed him" (1 Kings 19:18).

Right under our noses, there is a flurry of supernatural activity. Despairing Americans are beginning to utter prayers they never imagined they could say. Simultaneously, Christians are feeling an inner fire they have never felt before.

THE RISE OF THE WOUNDED HEALERS

Some of those who are rising up feel disqualified. The church has marginalized them. Yet they are a new breed of weapon about to emerge. They are wounded healers.

Who are these wounded healers? They don't have every hair in place or a clean record. They are not the sanitized, immaculate version of the body of Christ. They have messed up and then got back up. They were trampled and left for dead, and God restored them! They have no image to protect or ego to wound. They are the most dangerous people that Satan will ever face!

They gained all-new appetites in the furnace of affliction. They do not need the glory, and they eschew titles and awards. Their unswerving passion is to show compassion and take prisoners of love. You cannot get them to fight over doctrine because they have been to the cross. They know the blood that bought them and brought them back to life.

They are like Peter at Pentecost. Only a soul who has been handed another chance after denying the Lord three times will understand the inner fire of a wounded healer.

Who could write such a dangerous song as *Amazing Grace* but John Newton, whose epitaph says, "Once an infidel and libertine, a servant of slaves in Africa, was by the rich mercy of our LORD and SAVIOUR JESUS CHRIST preserved, restored, pardoned and appointed to preach the faith he had long laboured to destroy."[2]

You cannot find such zeal in religious do-gooders who never brave beyond ivied halls of respectability. You will not find this flame in the bleachers where those cold souls sit and keep score but will never take the field.

Wounded healers do not boast of clean uniforms and battles evaded but of scars and gates of hell invaded. They have no preaching pedigree but only a song that sets the captive free.

We all know Daniel 11:32, which says, "Those who do wickedly against the covenant he shall corrupt with flattery; but the people who know their God shall be strong, and carry out great exploits." But we tend to overlook what it says three verses later. Verse 35 says, "And some of those of understanding shall fall, to refine them, purify them, and make them white, until the time of the end; because it is still for the appointed time."

This verse is for wounded healers! Their attack is not to destroy them but to refine them! Their rejection and abandonment are not meant for shame but purity. It does not matter how their garments appear to Pharisees—only that they are white before God. Religious voices may have disqualified them, but their destiny is yet for an appointed time! The door that God holds open stays open!

Wounded healers can reach the masses that the regular church cannot. This makes them the perfect weapon for this moment, at the end of all things. If only these special-ops believers could see who they are and lose their need for the approval of cookie-cutter Christians, they would become God's tractor beam for lost souls.

The principal prize a wounded healer gains through their adversity is losing the fear of man. Many wounded healers have written to me about the horrific events of their lives, and in the face of everything else it became so real how God meant everything and the approval of their judges meant nothing. Truly, they shouted, "If God is for us, who can be against us!" (Rom. 8:31).

Many have written to me of the life of power that rose out of the ashes of despair. They felt equipped to do more than ever. They felt useful to God and lethal to the enemy! This must be the purest meaning of 2 Corinthians 1:3–4: "Blessed be the God and Father of our Lord Jesus Christ, the Father of mercies and God of all comfort, who comforts us in all our tribulation, that we may be able to comfort those who are in any trouble, with the comfort with which we ourselves are comforted by God."

I see this new generation of wounded healers coming to the fore. They do not wait for committee approval. They rent a school auditorium in a bad area and just start preaching. They preach raw sermons with an open heart, and crowds come from everywhere. Their frontline ministry is unlisted in the who's who of the Council of Churches, but Jesus feels just fine showing up every time they meet!

I see those who carry "unlicensed weapons," spiritually speaking. They open their homes to youth. They send out food, clothes, and love in the most unconventional ways imaginable, all with the smile of God.

Wounded healers might not wear denominational labels. They don't schmooze in the right rooms, but they carry the fight to where it matters the most. They operate under the direct orders of the King of kings!

When you see one, you will know it. They will not judge you, no matter how far gone you feel. They will see you through the lens of the Holy Spirit. They will see you as you will look after your miracle has come. You will feel welcome in their presence and look priceless in their eyes. They do not view the sinner as a commodity but as kidnapped royalty.

What about you? What will you do with your adversity, pain, and shame? All I can do is tell you what I did. At the lowest point of my life, God was waiting for me to make a choice. I chose to minister wherever the door opened and to preach as if each message were my last.

Deciding to go on when you feel nothing but agony is the greatest victory you will ever win. Not caring who gets the credit will rip the lid off your limits.

What are you and I waiting for? We have loved ones to snatch back! We have miracles to unleash on lost souls. There is a whole world that has never even heard of church fights or legalistic regulations.

When Elijah told the widow to get as many containers as possible and God filled them with oil, she realized the condition of the jars and pots was unimportant. God put oil in all of them. Wounded healers are not perfect containers; they are simply full of oil, and that is all that matters.

God knows what He is doing. Saul of Tarsus was the wounded

healer who surpassed all the twelve disciples. He felt unworthy to be a disciple and said so in no uncertain terms. Yet he attributed his unsurpassed labor for Christ to his awareness that he was a broken vessel.

Jesus showed another power of the wounded healer in Luke 7:44–47:

> Then He turned to the woman and said to Simon [the Pharisee], "Do you see this woman? I entered your house; you gave Me no water for My feet, but she has washed My feet with her tears and wiped them with the hair of her head. You gave Me no kiss, but this woman has not ceased to kiss My feet since the time I came in. You did not anoint My head with oil, but this woman has anointed My feet with fragrant oil. Therefore I say to you, her sins, which are many, are forgiven, for she loved much. But to whom little is forgiven, the same loves little."

Therefore, to all you misfits, I say you will not get credit from the religious peanut gallery, so you will have to be content with accomplishing more than any of them will for Christ and loving the Lord more than they can ever imagine!

Chapter 9

THE GREATEST REASON

OF ALL THE factors that will cause mass conversions, this next one is by far the greatest. Wait, how can it transcend the effect of mass misery? Or a panic over what the Woke mob is doing to our children? What about youth suddenly leaving Woke mentality behind? What about a massive army rising from within the church to gather the harvest?

Consider that all four factors existed in one form or another in Israel at the time of Ahab and Jezebel. The people had the same misery. I am sure they had disillusioned youth. I believe that is the reason Elijah asked why they halted between two opinions. Many of them were not convinced Baal was real. They were terrorized into believing in him.

They too must have reached a point of horror about throwing children into the fires of Baal. And finally, there were the seven thousand that God kept to Himself, who had not bowed the knee to Baal.

But none of those things touched off the miracle. The one that did is the one we will examine now.

French poet and novelist Victor Hugo is credited with the phrase "Nothing is more powerful than an idea whose time has come."[1] I would like to modify that statement. I can assure you there is nothing as powerful as a God idea whose time has come. The highest aspirations of the mightiest leaders on earth melt before the plan of God.

"And this is the plan: At the right time He will bring everything together under the authority of Christ—everything in heaven and on earth" (Eph. 1:10, NLT). All the pieces are coming together to bring everything under Christ's authority for this harvest at the right time.

It is God's time. The fire on Mount Carmel worked because God said, "Go." Remember 1 Kings 18:1: "And it came to pass after many days that the word of the LORD came to Elijah, in the third year, saying, 'Go, present yourself to Ahab, and I will send rain on the earth.'"

It is time. And when God says it's time, victory is a foregone conclusion. This factor is not greater simply because it can outdo the other factors. It is greater because it carries an assurance—from the highest authority—that the miracle is coming.

Throughout history this one factor has drained the life out of Satan more than any other. Look at him. He builds his most elaborate and intricate plots, only to have them go up in smoke—simply because God says it's time for them to go up in smoke. When God says it's over, it's over.

The greatest moment of Elijah's life was not when the fire fell on the sacrifice—it was when Jehovah said, "It is time."

How can we know it is God's time? That is a powerful question. And the answer can feel contradictory. But it's not.

Sometimes God tells us, but at other times He simply expects us to know. Let me give you an example. We have no record of God telling David it was time for him to kill the giant. But David tells us three times how he knew it was.

First, in 1 Samuel 17:26, "Then David spoke to the men who stood by him, saying, 'What shall be done for the man who kills this Philistine and takes away the reproach from Israel? For who is this uncircumcised Philistine, that he should defy the armies of the living God?'"

He tells us again in verse 36, "Your servant has killed both lion and bear; and this uncircumcised Philistine will be like one of them, seeing he has defied the armies of the living God."

Then he tells Goliath directly:

> You come to me with a sword, with a spear, and with a jav-
> elin. But I come to you in the name of the LORD of hosts, the
> God of the armies of Israel, whom you have defied. This day
> the LORD will deliver you into my hand, and I will strike you
> and take your head from you. And this day I will give the car-
> casses of the camp of the Philistines to the birds of the air and
> the wild beasts of the earth, that all the earth may know that
> there is a God in Israel. Then all this assembly shall know that
> the LORD does not save with sword and spear; for the battle is
> the LORD's, and He will give you into our hands.
>
> —1 SAMUEL 17:45–47

David understood that when evil crosses the line, it is time. No one said it more clearly than the psalmist, who wrote, "It is time for You to act, O LORD, for they have regarded Your law as void" (Ps. 119:126).

Why do I bring this up? Because I believe it addresses a great sin in the modern church. It is amazing how much evil we can live with. It is shocking the theologies we invent to avoid action against evil.

Think of an entire army frozen in fear, passively enduring the insults of Goliath. Anyone could have acted, and they would have seen the anointing of deliverance at work in them, just as David did.

But David was ready. He was in training for this even when he was unaware. Let's rehearse his training.

> But David said to Saul, "Your servant used to keep his father's
> sheep, and when a lion or a bear came and took a lamb out
> of the flock, I went out after it and struck it, and delivered
> the lamb from its mouth; and when it arose against me, I
> caught it by its beard, and struck and killed it. Your ser-
> vant has killed both lion and bear; and this uncircumcised

Philistine will be like one of them, seeing he has defied the
armies of the living God."

—1 SAMUEL 17:34–36

David's training was not simply that he killed a lion and a bear.
It goes much deeper. He did not stop and think about what to do
when the lamb was in the lion's jaws. Instinctively he attacked! He
attacked the bear in the same way. He never doubted or hesitated.

When David said, "This uncircumcised Philistine will be like
one of them," we miss the similarity. This goes deeper than just
that Goliath *defied* the armies of the living God. David is saying,
"This is just like the times that lions and bears came after my sheep.
It's not something I need to think about. I need to act!"

It was time for the church to act before school prayer was banned
on June 25, 1962. It was God's time before January 22, 1973, when
abortion was legalized. It was God's time before June 26, 2015, when
the biblical definition of marriage died in the Supreme Court.

But you will say, "Mario, didn't you tell us that Elijah had to
wait? Didn't he spend three and a half years waiting?" He couldn't
have acted until God said it was time, right?

This mystery is solved by looking at Esther.

> Then Mordecai told them to reply to Esther, "Do not imagine
> that you in the king's palace can escape any more than all
> the Jews. For if you remain silent at this time, liberation and
> rescue will arise for the Jews from another place, and you
> and your father's house will perish [since you did not help
> when you had the chance]. And who knows whether you
> have attained royalty for such a time as this [and for this very
> purpose]?"
>
> —ESTHER 4:13–14, AMP

These verses prove one thing right off the top. A vessel can be
chosen and fail to fulfill its mission. But the ultimate danger is not
to the mission. Mordecai tells Esther that deliverance will come

from another place. It is certain that God will have His way, but she and her father's house will be destroyed.

Then Mordecai gives the chilling reason for punishment: "since you did not help when you had the chance."

On June 24, 2022, *Roe v. Wade* was finally overturned—long after it should have been. God will find a way. Not only was the battle longer than it should have been, but also many pastors added insult to injury. They stood in their pulpits and said, "We should not be celebrating."

People's willingness to volunteer is one of the greatest signals that this is God's time. They make themselves available to confront evil. Elijah saw the glorious miracle because he made himself available. That is the day I believe we have entered. But God is indeed separating the sheep from the goats.

CHRONOS AND KAIROS

To make the urgent point of this chapter, I must reference the two Greek words used in the New Testament to signify time. They are *chronos* and *kairos*. The first refers to a season, and the second refers to a moment.

God's call is just like that. God will say, "It is time [*chronos*]," as in, "You are called to enter a season of preparation." To God this is a most critical time.

Then comes the decisive moment [*kairos*]. *Merriam-Webster* defines *kairos* as "a time when conditions are right for the accomplishment of a crucial action: the opportune and decisive moment."[2]

The concept originates in the practice of Greek archery, representing the moment when the archer finds the perfect opening to shoot his arrow and hit his target.

It is easy to see that Esther began her season when she entered the palace to prepare to see the king. Likewise, Elijah entered his season right after he declared the drought. In both cases they are essentially hidden.

Why is this so important to know? Because America has fallen into moral disaster not just because of evil politicians but because of unavailable Christians. A passive attitude brought us to the brink of disaster.

Time and time again, God has reached out to the American church and sought someone to stand in the gap. Ezekiel 22:30 says, "So I sought for a man among them who would make a wall, and stand in the gap before Me on behalf of the land, that I should not destroy it; but I found no one."

My point is this: many among the current crop of preachers and Christian leaders will answer to God for insulting Him by asking for guidance over things that are more than obvious. It is a special wickedness when we make something optional that the Bible declares mandatory.

This spirit of deception came on Balaam. He had a gift of prophecy, but he was corrupted. A king hired him to put a curse on Israel, assuming it would help defeat the Jews. Here is what happened when the prophet prayed for permission:

> So Balaam said to God, "Balak the son of Zippor, king of Moab, has sent to me, saying, 'Look, a people has come out of Egypt, and they cover the face of the earth. Come now, curse them for me; perhaps I shall be able to overpower them and drive them out.'" And God said to Balaam, "You shall not go with them; you shall not curse the people, for they are blessed."
> —NUMBERS 22:10–12

That should have ended it, right? No, it did not. The king raised the ante, and Balaam took the bait. He even tried to act virtuously. But it is the last phrase that tells the story. See if you catch it.

> Then Balaam answered and said to the servants of Balak, "Though Balak were to give me his house full of silver and gold, I could not go beyond the word of the LORD my God,

to do less or more. Now therefore, please, you also stay here
tonight, that I may know what more the LORD will say to me."
—NUMBERS 22:18–19

When Balaam asked God a second time to see if He would
change His mind, he incurred the wrath of God. God granted permission—not to enrich him but to kill him.

How dark and despicable it is that some of our spiritual leaders
claim either that they did not know they should address the wickedness of the land or they are not called to do so—or worse, that they
have permission to do this! How are they any better than Balaam?

But there is a miracle at work in the land. It is God's time. Our
national *kairos* moment will arrive. I believe it is soon.

Now I must explain why I am excited even amid so much evil
and compromise.

In cities across America, people that no one has heard of are
being strangely quickened. They may not have any idea that their
season of frustration—like Elijah's in the wilderness—was forging
them for the astonishing harvest.

Who can stop them? No one can. What will be their assignment? Souls, souls, and more souls. We will win them in the slums.
We will win them in the mansions, schools, businesses, airports,
prisons, hospitals, offices, and anywhere else hurting, despairing
people suffer in darkness.

Because it is God's time, we will see great signs and wonders.
They will be pure and free of the abuses they have long endured.
Because it is God's time, this new breed will possess pure hearts
and pure motives. Churches will rise to heights of glory, fire, and
love. They will grow because society sees Jesus at work in them.

I have tried to tell you why it's our turn now. I have also tried to
show you the factors at work in Americans, making them ripe for
harvest. But we still have a big issue: How can we prepare not to fail
when our moment comes?

It is no good to awaken yourself to hope and excite your spirit about these coming events if you do not understand your calling or are not completely devoted to your preparation.

We need to enter a school of the Holy Spirit that will make us fit to seize our moment when it arrives.

There are some urgent points to cover. We must revisit prayer in a new and living way. We must experience prayer in a way that makes us wonder if we have ever prayed.

Along with this, we must receive fresh fire. Yes, you may have received the baptism in the Holy Spirit, but that is not your final outpouring. You must have fresh overflows of fire and power that burn out the habits that try to reclaim you. You must have this so the words that will cut evil like a sword can be trusted to be in your mouth.

That, my friend, is where we are going from here. It is God's time for you to become the weapon you have always wanted to be so that you may stand and deliver your part in this, the greatest of all harvests.

PART III:

TRAINING TO TAKE YOUR TURN

T RAINING REDUCES FEAR. Identity releases confidence. Here are the practical instructions that will give us the skills to reap the harvest.

Chapter 10

HAVE YOU DECIDED IT'S YOUR TURN?

C HAPTER 1 GAVE us a natural example of someone taking their turn. Chapter 2 gave us the supernatural example of someone taking their turn. I have talked about Kirk Gibson. I have talked about Elijah. Now let's talk about you.

Have you decided it's your turn now? This cannot be a light decision. It must be from the core of your being. Unless it is, none of the training will stick, and you will not act on what you have learned. Without an irrevocable decision, the power will not come and the fire will not fall.

To be stirred but not changed makes you no different from the millions of Americans who call themselves Christian. They agree there's a problem. They believe something should be done. They may even be fooling themselves and thinking they are doing something. But they are unavailable and therefore disqualified.

The book title says it is our turn now. But honestly, it is not everyone's turn. We know God will use people in this massive opportunity. But who are they? In Matthew 22:14 we are told that "many are called, but few are chosen."

The scriptural context is important. So let's see the context of that verse to understand who is called and who is chosen.

> But when the king came in to see the guests, he saw a man there who did not have on a wedding garment. So he said to him, "Friend, how did you come in here without a wedding

garment?" And he was speechless. Then the king said to the servants, "Bind him hand and foot, take him away, and cast him into outer darkness; there will be weeping and gnashing of teeth." For many are called, but few are chosen.

—MATTHEW 22:11–14

Jesus' reference to the man building on sand or the seed falling on hard ground represents a person who heard the Word but did not take it to heart. Wearing the required wedding garb says that you understand and honor the ceremony. This man did the unthinkable. By not wearing a wedding garment, he disrespected the event. He treated it as if it were common. He was invited, but because of his insult he was rejected.

Similarly, another call goes out to the general Christian population, not to a wedding but to a mission: Who will march in and harvest the vast field of souls? Who will go and save a nation? Indeed, many are called, but only those who hear and respond correctly are chosen.

Eli the priest, though corrupt, could still tell young Samuel how to respond to God's voice.

And the LORD called Samuel again the third time. So, he arose and went to Eli, and said, "Here I am, for you did call me." Then Eli perceived that the LORD had called the boy. Therefore Eli said to Samuel, "Go, lie down; and it shall be, if He calls you, that you must say, 'Speak, LORD, for Your servant hears.'"

—1 SAMUEL 3:8–9

Samuel did what Eli said, and a new era dawned on Israel.

Who is called, and who is chosen? The answer is so simple and clear that we stumble over it. The *called* who are willing to pay the price become the *chosen.* Many hear the call and are excited about it until they see the cost and disqualify themselves.

Notice that Eli instructed the boy to include the word *servant* the next time God spoke. That is a mouthful! Until then, Samuel had been saying, "You called me," which can mean, "What do you want?" But saying, "Speak, Lord, for Your *servant* hears," means "I will do what You want."

Every Bible hero has this in common: they gladly did what God ordered them to do in the face of insurmountable obstacles and losing everything. The Bible teems with stories about the few who paid the price. You can even say that *paying the price* is key in every Bible story. This truth is a matter of life and death right now!

Without a massive surge of unselfish service, our nation is doomed. And that brings us to the great disaster: self-denial is unpopular now. The modern church has been groomed against sacrifice and service.

Think of it! In a time when we need servants most, we are least likely to get them. When it is like this, you know the devil is behind it.

Two critical imbalances put the church in this condition. I have talked about them before, but now we see them in depth. The two imbalances are

1. the focus of megachurches to fill seats, and

2. Spirit-filled groups bent toward mystical and emotional experiences.

The first imbalance is bad because it keeps soldiers off the battlefield. The second is even worse because it sends soldiers onto a fantasy battlefield. The first group does not know the Bible. The second takes the Bible out of context.

Let us focus on the first extreme of filling seats. Their idea was to create a wide on-ramp to church and formulate a palatable message. Marketing replaced prayer and dependence on the Holy Spirit. They would not declare Christianity: they would sell it. And like any good salesforce, they would allow the audience to help create the message. They relied on polls, focus groups, and consultants to create "Christianity incorporated."

As a result, big churches were overrun by weak members who could not make a difference, did not know what they believed, and were powerless to stand against the contamination of culture. As soon as leaders enticed people into the church, they ruined any chance to teach them to serve.

Clearly, the Bible warned us this mutation was coming: "...having a form of godliness but denying its power. And from such people turn away!" (2 Tim. 3:5).

The second imbalance is in the Spirit-filled community, where they play with signs, wonders, and the prophetic. As with the first extreme, compromised preaching keeps believers off the battlefield. But in the second extreme false prophets and apostles send believers onto a fantasy battlefield.

Make no mistake, miracles are real. They are flowing through many ministries. There is a true gift of prophecy. The problem is that social media has created a swamp for self-proclaimed prophets and apostles. I have noticed that the real ones eschew titles and just function in their gift.

The fakes awakened an unnatural appetite in the body of Christ. They set believers on a course to run after prophetic words instead of reading the Bible. False prophets set up websites to offer people daily prophetic words—like a Christian horoscope.

They continually feast on preposterous visions, dreams, and visits to heaven. There is no way this movement leads to soul winning or national revival. They are too busy having out-of-Bible experiences.

Remember that I said the second imbalance takes Scripture out of context? Here is an example: those who believe in endlessly singing repetitive phrases—claiming it will save souls and bring revival—justify it by abusing John 12:32: "And I, if I am lifted up from the earth, will draw all peoples to Myself." But that is not how Jesus draws all men.

All they had to do was read the next verse! So here they are together in context: "And I, if I am lifted up from the earth, will draw all peoples to Myself. This He said, signifying by what death He would die" (vv. 32–33).

It is His death on the cross that draws all men. But people ask, "How can anyone speak against worship?" Do you see how that works? The enemy chooses a sacred act and turns it into a sacred cow so we will not go and win lost souls or cry out against evil to save a nation.

Leaving our safe places to go out in power *is* an act of worship. It glorifies God! "By this My Father is glorified, that you bear much fruit; so you will be My disciples" (John 15:8).

The bottom line is that the enemy has used both extremes to create distracted, self-centered converts. They have been conditioned to believe in a God who responds to their every whim. This is not the God of the Bible.

The Bible is victimized in both deviations from the truth. In the first, we see the Bible redacted to suit the audience. In the second, we see prophetic words elevated to an equal and even greater status than Scripture to suit the audience.

The power of the audience to create false teachers cannot be overstated. It is clever of the enemy to get us to misread these verses:

> For the time will come when they will not endure sound doctrine, but according to their own desires, because they have itching ears, they will heap up for themselves teachers; and they will turn their ears away from the truth, and be turned aside to fables.
>
> —2 TIMOTHY 4:3–4

Whenever someone preaches from these verses, they assume it is a warning to the audience about false teachers; however, *it is a warning to preachers about false audiences.* Read it again. You'll see the audience has itching ears.

Nevertheless, these leaders took matters into their own hands. They stopped relying on the Holy Spirit. They wanted people for themselves and not to advance the kingdom of God. And the people's adoration kept them going in the wrong direction.

Many of the people in these movements came out of solid churches. Many left to seek some lukewarm religious resort to hide in. Others came out from under the care of true shepherds because they wanted an exotic experience.

The devil did all this on purpose. He did it out of desperation. I liken it to the situation in the Old Testament when Israel was subject to the Philistines. And to blunt the threat of a Jewish uprising, the Philistines destroyed all the forges to prevent them from making weapons.

> Now there was no blacksmith to be found throughout all the land of Israel, for the Philistines said, "Lest the Hebrews make swords or spears." But all the Israelites would go down to the Philistines to sharpen each man's plowshare, his mattock, his ax, and his sickle.
>
> —1 Samuel 13:19–20

The excesses and mistakes of the modern church closed the forges. Through distraction and deception, the church lost the power to make the very weapons we need right now.

> For the weapons of our warfare are not carnal but mighty in God for pulling down strongholds, casting down arguments and every high thing that exalts itself against the knowledge of God, bringing every thought into captivity to the obedience of Christ.
>
> —2 Corinthians 10:4–5

So is there any hope of building an army? Whose turn is it to write new pages of church history? Who will rise in Christ's name and thrust the sword of the Lord into the heart of darkness? Will the Lord of the harvest find needed workers now that the doors are flying open to win souls? *Yes, He will!*

Nobody builds an army better. No one else can take the improbable and equip them to do the impossible. And I can tell you the profile of those chosen for the glorious task ahead.

So whose turn is it? I can tell you with absolute conviction. It is your turn if you can say yes to any of the following:

- Your love for your children and grandchildren is greater than your fear of what anyone thinks of you. You are so concerned about the world they will live in after you are gone that you are willing to pay the price to protect their future.

- You know why crime is rising and morals are falling. You know who is stealing our freedoms and our way of life. And you are willing to do everything God says to stop them.

- You are frustrated. And you have no idea how perfect that frustration is for what the Holy Spirit will do in you next.

- You are in the radical middle. You are not fooled by the entertainment model of church or the hyperemotional church.

- You are young with many friends, but you feel alone. Your peers don't get you. You feel like their plans are so shallow compared with what you see.

- You are among a special group. The people of God have been talking among themselves. They have compared notes. They left Christian events shaking their heads, saying, "This is not it." They are sick of the grandiose, showy projects of egoistic ministers. They are done with gatherings that feature smoke and mirrors but cannot potentially stop the national disaster.

- You are hearing God say clear and precise things to you. And you are stunned that you keep bumping into people you have never met before who are hearing the same thing.

How do you begin to take your turn? The first step is separation. You are overtaken by a clear sense of the things you will never do again and things you will never be part of again. It begins now. Your road map is found in these verses:

> But in a great house there are not only vessels of gold and silver, but also of wood and clay, some for honor and some for dishonor. Therefore if anyone cleanses himself from the latter, he will be a vessel for honor, sanctified and useful for the Master, prepared for every good work.
>
> —2 Timothy 2:20–21

The family of God is vast. Paul has no illusions that everyone in it is right with God. He even calls some in the family dishonorable. But then he offers an incredible promise to some in the house. However, that promise carries a condition: *if* you cleanse yourself from these.

That can seem harsh. It is saying to wash off the residue of compromised and foolish people. You must separate from Christianity incorporated and the haunted mansion.

Think of an eagle with amnesia. Someone convinced him that he was a turkey. He is in the yard pecking at grain and fighting nausea. He can't help but stare at the sky and wonder what those deep longings are all about. He can't bring himself to be excited about the things the rest of the turkeys are interested in. Then he remembers what he is and where he belongs, and *whoosh*! He is gone.

You picked up this book because you have those longings that can't be fulfilled here. You must leave the turkey yard, spit out the corn, and find the sincere meat of the Word of God. And get ready to do battle.

You now stand where heroic vessels of God and patriots have stood before. It is time for you to leave the artificial, the spurious, the powerless, and the cowardly.

Whose turn is it? A. W. Tozer described them:

> [They] will serve God and mankind from motives too high to be understood by the rank and file of religious retainers who today shuttle in and out of the sanctuary. They will make no decisions out of fear, take no course out of a desire to please, accept no service for financial considerations, perform no religious act out of mere custom; nor will they allow themselves to be influenced by the love of publicity or the desire for reputation.[1]

Chapter 11

YOU BELONG AT THE
TABLE OF INFLUENCE

NOTHING IN THIS book will help you unless you believe you belong at the table of influence. Why bother to excite your heart about changing America if, in the end, you remain a spectator?

Why arm yourself with information you will never use? Why even talk about what's wrong with our nation? That makes you the proverbial tree that fell in the woods.

Your voice must not just be raised. It must be heard.

To take a seat at the table of influence is an act of defiance. You are challenging the systematic censorship of the gospel. You are declaring that our nation is founded on the teachings of Jesus.

We need to define the table because apparently a lot happens at the table!

- "If we can get both sides to the table"—a place to meet to negotiate or discuss how to resolve a particular issue or situation.

- "That is off the table"—to be withdrawn or no longer available, as for consideration, acceptance, discussion, and so forth.

- "Pay me under the table"—paying an employee under the table means they get paid off the record.

- "What do you bring to the table?"—What money, influence, or talent can you offer?"

- "I am turning the tables on you"—to reverse one's position relative to someone else, especially by turning a position of disadvantage into one of advantage.

Except for getting paid under the table, you will have a role in all those table activities.

The first stage is to be convinced you belong at the table. This work is done inside you. It has nothing to do with changing your circumstances or waiting for an opportunity. It is all about identity.

Get this: If you do not believe you belong at the table of influence, no one else will either.

Numbers 13:33 says, "There we saw the giants (the descendants of Anak came from the giants); and we were like grasshoppers in our own sight, and so we were in their sight." How you see yourself is how the enemy sees you.

The fire fell on Mount Carmel to confirm two identities: God's and the man of God's.

> And it came to pass, at the time of the offering of the evening sacrifice, that Elijah the prophet came near and said, "LORD God of Abraham, Isaac, and Israel, let it be known this day that You are God in Israel and I am Your servant, and that I have done all these things at Your word."
>
> —1 KINGS 18:36

The identity you need to sit at the table of influence comes from the Holy Spirit. Before the fire falls on your Mount Carmel, it must fall on you.

The prophet Samuel tells us how our identity is transformed when he says to Saul, "Then the Spirit of the LORD will come upon you, and you will prophesy with them and be turned into another man. And let it be, when these signs come to you, that you do as the occasion demands; for God is with you" (1 Sam. 10:6–7).

Notice the natural outcome of the God-given identity: you will do what the occasion demands—for God is with you.

If anyone ever felt inadequate to do what the occasion demanded, it was Joshua. His identity crisis was a double-edged sword. First, he was replacing the legend of all time, Moses. Second, Joshua was leading two million unruly people.

God didn't begin by granting Joshua talent, wisdom, or even courage. God gave him an identity and forcefully commanded him to accept it. God had to convince Joshua he belonged in this role. He was the rightful leader of Israel. And at the risk of being redundant, I must say, if Joshua did not believe it, the people would not either.

Behold the lengths to which Jehovah goes to infuse identity and confidence in Joshua.

> After the death of Moses the servant of the LORD, it came to pass that the LORD spoke to Joshua the son of Nun, Moses' assistant, saying: "Moses My servant is dead. Now therefore, arise, go over this Jordan, you and all this people, to the land which I am giving to them—the children of Israel. Every place that the sole of your foot will tread upon I have given you, as I said to Moses. From the wilderness and this Lebanon as far as the great river, the River Euphrates, all the land of the Hittites, and to the Great Sea toward the going down of the sun, shall be your territory. No man shall be able to stand before you all the days of your life; as I was with Moses, so I will be with you. I will not leave you nor forsake you. Be strong and of good courage, for to this people you shall divide as an inheritance the land which I swore to their fathers to give them. Only be strong and very courageous, that you may observe to do according to all the law which Moses My servant commanded you; do not turn from it to the right hand or to the left, that you may prosper wherever you go. This Book of the

Law shall not depart from your mouth, but you shall meditate in it day and night, that you may observe to do according to all that is written in it. For then you will make your way prosperous, and then you will have good success. Have I not commanded you? Be strong and of good courage; do not be afraid, nor be dismayed, for the LORD your God is with you wherever you go."

—JOSHUA 1:1–9

You are not a gate crasher posing as an invited guest at the table. You have every right to be there. You are supposed to exert great influence.

However, if preachers use the term *influence* today, they risk being labeled dominionists. I need to say this: I do not agree with dominion theology. I do not see anywhere in the Bible where we take over the earth and present it as a prize to God.

I am not a dominionist; I am an evangelist. I am not here to colonize the earth; I am here to evangelize the earth. It is foolish to believe we can set up a theocracy to legislate morality. People do not become moral by enforcing the law on them. They are transformed by a change of heart.

The Bible is clear on this. Romans 8:7 says, "Because the carnal mind is enmity against God; for it is not subject to the law of God, nor indeed can be."

But it is equally foolish not to use our authority where we can. I can't legislate morality, but I can certainly fight to stop others from legislating immorality. This takes us to our next urgent discovery.

We must not just believe we belong at the table. We must believe in the message we bring to the table. The gospel is the greatest message the world has ever heard. Paul declared, "For I am not ashamed of the gospel of Christ, for it is the power of God unto salvation for everyone who believes, for the Jew first and also for the Greek" (Rom. 1:16).

If there is a part of history Satan most wants to bury, it is this: the towering impact of the gospel of Jesus Christ on humanity. Nothing comes close. There is not a human ill it has not touched. Nothing else removes suicide, addiction, racism, hatred, guilt, shame, and perversion like the gospel of Jesus Christ.

Just as we vehemently reject the false labels they try to put on our identity, so must we repudiate the branding of the gospel by Wokeism. It is garbage to say our faith is part of the patriarchal system of oppression.

I will go further. The benefit of Christ on humanity is so pervasive and effective for good that we can issue the following challenge: If you leave Jesus out, then I question your sincerity about abolishing racism. If you do not consider Jesus, I wonder whether you truly care about women's rights. If you have a heart for the poor, the dying, and the oppressed but say nothing of what Christ has done for the human heart, you are only posing as a liberator.

Trying to turn a miracle into a crime is not new. Let's look at the label, the evil, and how Peter refuses to back down.

Here is what happens: the crippled beggar at the gate called Beautiful—known to the entire city of Jerusalem—gets up and walks, which causes a glorious uproar, and many are converted. Peter is arrested and ordered to appear before the same leaders who condemned Jesus to death.

> And it came to pass, on the next day, that their rulers, elders, and scribes, as well as Annas the high priest, Caiaphas, John, and Alexander, and as many as were of the family of the high priest, were gathered together at Jerusalem. And when they had set them in the midst, they asked, "By what power or by what name have you done this?"
>
> —ACTS 4:5–7

Peter's arrest and the tone of the question show us that they are branding the miracle a crime. As we will see, evil is bottomless when its power is threatened.

But Peter is not having it. He goes out of his way to tear their label off and call it by its right name. In verses 8–10 we read:

> Then Peter, filled with the Holy Spirit, said to them, "Rulers of the people and elders of Israel: If we this day are judged for a good deed done to a helpless man, by what means he has been made well, let it be known to you all, and to all the people of Israel, that by the name of Jesus Christ of Nazareth, whom you crucified, whom God raised from the dead, by Him this man stands here before you whole."

It is not a crime. It is a good deed! They were criminalizing the best thing there is: a miracle. When the Woke crowd labels Christianity racist, criminal, and obsolete, they are calling the gospel the opposite of what it truly is: the best news the world has ever heard. We must not let this happen to us. We belong at the table of influence, showing them what we bring to the table.

Next, Peter lowers the boom in verses 11–12.

> This is the "stone which was rejected by you builders, which has become the chief cornerstone." Nor is there salvation in any other, for there is no other name under heaven given among men by which we must be saved.

We must not be afraid to call evil leaders out for the villains they are. Peter invoked a verse from the Old Testament that predicted a future crime—not just any crime but a high crime. He was telling them they were the evildoers prophesied in Psalm 118:22–23.

> The stone which the builders rejected has become the chief cornerstone. This was the LORD's doing; it is marvelous in our eyes.

This is called turning the tables. They arrested Peter, and he revealed the fact that they committed the crime of murdering the Messiah.

Yes, we must be loving. But we must also stare down evil and call it out. We must throw it back. Let's look again at how Elijah did that.

Remember that Ahab was blaming the man of God for the drought (an act so Woke as not to be denied). How absurd! It was Jezebel and Ahab who brought all this misery upon Israel.

> Then it happened, when Ahab saw Elijah, that Ahab said to him, "Is that you, O troubler of Israel?" And he answered, "I have not troubled Israel, but you and your father's house have, in that you have forsaken the commandments of the LORD and have followed the Baals."
>
> —1 KINGS 18:17–18

Elijah turned the tables, which is what we must do. But we are up against an astonishing evil. Peter saw that evil. I want you to see it too.

> Now when they saw the boldness of Peter and John, and perceived that they were uneducated and untrained men, they marveled. And they realized that they had been with Jesus. And seeing the man who had been healed standing with them, they could say nothing against it. But when they had commanded them to go aside out of the council, they conferred among themselves, saying, "What shall we do to these men? For, indeed, that a notable miracle has been done through them is evident to all who dwell in Jerusalem, and we cannot deny it."
>
> —ACTS 4:13–16

Let's look closely at what they realized and said. "This miracle is real. God did it. Everybody knows it. We can't deny it." So what did they do in the face of such overpowering truth and the undeniable fact that they were opposing God Himself? They tried to stop it!

> But so that it spreads no further among the people, let us severely threaten them, that from now on they speak to no man in this name.
>
> —ACTS 4:17

They should have realized this and said, "Gentlemen, what we have here is a miracle. This is what our people have yearned for ever since Abraham. We have before us a miracle of healing and a message of hope for all we dread. Let us embrace it and live in the glow and blessing of what God has done!"

That is the depth of evil you and I face at the table. But we must resist it. We must not let anything stop us from sitting at the table of influence. "If God is for us, who can be against us?" (Rom. 8:31).

Not only must we highlight the surpassing power of the gospel, but also we must expose the utter bankruptcy of Wokeness. One without the other will never work. We cannot declare God's love without exposing the extremity of our national sins.

What do we bring to the table? Absolute proof of the power and love of Jesus. We are not a vague movement with a murky message. We are the bona fide children of God with a message of hope and power brighter than the sun!

Now that you know you belong at the table of influence, let's look at three things you must do to take your turn.

CHAPTER 12

THREE THINGS YOU MUST DO TO TAKE YOUR TURN

G OD CANNOT SPEAK through you today unless you realize three things.

1. You must publicly oppose evil.

2. You must not wait to win souls, because the harvest is already here.

3. You must not wait for the lukewarm church.

1. Speak out against evil.

You are locked in a battle between good and evil, and no one is neutral in this war. Those who believe they are neutral unwittingly advance evil. Silence always helps the oppressor.

Elie Wiesel, the Romanian-born Holocaust survivor who became an American writer, professor, and political activist, said the following during his Nobel Peace Prize acceptance speech on December 10, 1986:

> We must always take sides. Neutrality helps the oppressor, never the victim. Silence encourages the tormentor, never the tormented. Sometimes we must interfere. When human lives are endangered, when human dignity is in jeopardy, national borders and sensitivities become irrelevant. Wherever men and women are persecuted because of their race, religion, or

political views, that place must—at that moment—become the center of the universe.[1]

The "center of our universe" today might look like the political arena, but we're fighting a spiritual problem, not a political one. We must recognize the evil forces controlling the actions of our leaders to destroy morality, freedom, love of country, and our children. At the risk of sounding divisive, I must agree with Elie Wiesel and challenge you that it is time to take sides.

What sides am I referring to? This book is not calling you to engage in a fight between Democrats and Republicans or Right and Left; it is a battle cry to rise up and take your place in the war between good and evil.

I may identify the other side with terms such as Woke, Left, or even Democrat, but I assure you that my opposition to their agenda is not political. That is because their agenda is not political. They are not a political party. They are oppressors.

They attack their enemies like oppressors. They imprison the innocent like oppressors. If you were to list their actions without bias, without the camouflage of the leftist media, you would see no difference between their actions and those of totalitarian regimes. I am not challenging you to oppose a political party; I'm imploring you to stand up against a criminal enterprise.

And there is no excuse for anyone who claims to love God to remain silent. When a fellow minister scolded me for "being political," I rebuked him. I said, "One day you will be forced to take sides—when depravity is overwhelming, children in your church are taken from their parents, and you are handed scripts of what you can and cannot preach. But by then it will be too late. You will not be seen as a brave hero. Patriots, freedom fighters, and devoted Christians will only see one thing about you: how very, very long it took you to join the fight."

No version of this moment calls for any Christian to sit on the bench. There is no deferment from this war. We must all preach the gospel—and we must all fight to protect our freedom to preach the gospel.

The only thing that should be fixed in your mind is the America you will leave behind for your children and grandchildren. We must do everything we can to stop the social prison being built for our children and grandchildren.

The old saying has never been truer: if you stay silent and fail to rock the boat in this war between good and evil, your life might be easier, but your children's won't. Thomas Paine was even clearer: "'If there must be trouble, let it be in my day, that my child may have peace'; and this single reflection, well applied, is sufficient to awaken every man to duty."[2]

Again, I'm not telling you to hate the Democratic Party; I'm asking you to stand strong against any group or person carrying out the agenda of evil. I wholeheartedly believe Psalm 94 includes us when it instructs us to declare moral war on them: "Who will rise up for me against the evildoers? Who will stand up for me against the workers of iniquity?" (Ps. 94:16).

No Christian can justify having anything to do with evil. Verse 20 tells us directly that God has nothing to do with them. It says, "Shall the throne of iniquity, which devises evil by law, have fellowship with You?"

The Amplified Bible, Classic Edition, renders Psalm 94:20 this way: "Shall the throne of iniquity have fellowship with You—they who frame and hide their unrighteous doings under [the sacred name of] law?"

Devising evil by law is exactly what we're witnessing in our day. We cannot legislate morality, but we must stop evildoers from legislating immorality.

Many of our leaders—including some in our pulpits—are guilty of the high crime of giving legitimacy to evil. In his commentary on Psalm 94, Matthew Henry said, "Iniquity is daring enough even when human laws are against it, which often prove too weak to give an effectual check to it; but how insolent, how mischievous, is it when it is backed by a law! Iniquity is not the better, but much the worse, for being enacted by law; nor will it excuse those that practise it to say that they did but do as they were bidden."[3]

Notice how Henry says we can't use the excuse that we were just obeying the law. That is why Dietrich Bonhoeffer said, "Silence in the face of evil is itself evil: God will not hold us guiltless. Not to speak is to speak. Not to act is to act."[4]

Two groups within the church tell us a big lie. They are the compromising Christians and lukewarm Christians who refuse to vote. Their big lie is that the Democrats are no worse than the Republicans. They use this as an excuse for siding with the Left or not voting at all.

Lest you think I'm telling you to be a Republican, their party's numbers are also replete with do-nothing career politicians (some call them RINOs). Too often they have chosen their own survival over the good of the nation. Many of them have rested on their laurels and even sided with evil.

We must rebuke anyone who is corrupt, who lies, or who compromises with evil, regardless of their political party. The body of Christ must not be their cheap date. We must hold their feet to the fire. They must fear us. They must feel our rage.

They need to be rebuked like the Pharisees in the Bible for their principal sin: *hypocrisy*! They are hypocrites, and we must rebuke them. In every instance where a compromising leader is running for office, they should be exposed and replaced by true conservatives who love America and the Constitution.

The Bible has a description for any Christian leader who mingles with corruption and hypocrisy and will not denounce evil. Proverbs 25:26 (AMPC) says, "Like a muddied fountain and a polluted spring is a righteous man who yields, falls down, and compromises his integrity before the wicked."

But for those who choose to stand and deliver, there are many promises of blessings. A rich reward awaits those who rebuke the wicked. Proverbs 24:25 says, "But those who rebuke the wicked will have delight, and a good blessing will come upon them."

2. Start winning souls now.

Now we must turn our attention to an equally urgent subject. We cannot wait to start winning souls. I believe the harvest is already here. I believe Satan is deceiving the church by giving it a false picture of the American public.

The church continues to misread the mood of Americans. It insists on assuming Americans hate God and will reject the gospel. The church believes the lie that we cannot confront and conquer the leftist agenda. The narrative of defeat is everywhere. Even in sermons intended to be victorious, there is the smell of defeat.

When messages from churches refuse to confront our culture's evil, they ignore the harvest. When their content is only for believers, they ignore the harvest. No matter how high-sounding and motivational the message, if it ignores the harvest, it is grounded in defeat.

Wake up, church! America—the real America—wants Jesus. They yearn for forgiveness and peace of mind. They do not hate our history. I am talking about your neighbor—from the kid at the park all alone to tax-paying, law-abiding citizens.

California is supposed to be the worst place in the world for the gospel. So then why did the number of conversions at our tent crusades in Fresno, Bakersfield, and Modesto, and at William Jessup University create a volunteer shortage crisis? We thought six hundred fervent volunteers in Modesto would be enough to handle those who gave their lives to Christ, but it was not! The harvest was bigger than we thought. Way bigger.

I do not harbor a fantasy that somehow I was so eloquent and powerful it broke the spell over these California cities. All the glory goes to God. The people were hungry, and they still are. They're hungry with a hunger that does not need bells and whistles or any kind of diluted message.

And the hunger in California should be a foreshadowing to us all. If it is like that there, what is it like where you live? What if vast numbers of Americans want God? What if we are so conditioned to believe they don't want God that we are sleeping through the harvest? Proverbs 10:5 tells us, "He who gathers in summer is a wise son; he who sleeps in harvest is a son who causes shame."

3. Do not wait for the lukewarm church.

The rumble of revival and reformation, the earthquake of American freedom, is all around you. It beckons you! Every atom of your being screams for you to join the wounded healers healing America. All the cells of your body vibrate with anticipation.

But you hesitate. You are hoping your lukewarm friends and other lukewarm Christians will change.

The tide is turning. Millions are ready to cast off the yoke of corruption. Voices rise in schools, corporate headquarters, and all the halls of power. Even leftist commentators and celebrities are defecting from their insane agendas.

Millions of Americans are yearning for a clear voice and a path back to freedom. You are one of those voices. It's time! Don't miss your turn trying to convince the lukewarm.

Everywhere preachers take a stand, their churches are growing. Their services radiate with the power of the Holy Spirit. Meanwhile, lukewarm cathedrals wallow in a plugged-up and contaminated creek of denial. I'll close this chapter by giving you five reasons you cannot afford to wait for your lukewarm Christian friends.

FIVE REASONS YOU CANNOT AFFORD TO WAIT

1. Your lukewarm friends and church are stealing your joy and hope for a new America.

Every time you get around them, they downplay your fervor and question your involvement in "politics." They wear you out with their lame excuses that betray reality. Their double standards are maddening. It drains you to hear them talk about how Trump hurt their feelings, but they have no feelings about your daughter sharing bathrooms and showers with males at school. They have no feelings for babies born alive who can now legally be set aside to die.

Stop letting them drain you! Get with the growing number who are pressing in for revival and freedom.

2. You will never change them.

They are bent on self-preservation. Their mission is to keep their club alive. The Bible doesn't matter to them. American history and the Constitution do not matter to them. The only thing that matters is to maintain their religious charade.

3. Jesus said to look to the fields.

John 4:35 declares, "Do you not say, 'There are still four months and then comes the harvest'? Behold, I say to you, lift up your eyes and look at the fields, for they are already white for harvest!"

Pastors should not be looking at how their preaching might offend hypocrites. They should be looking at the fields. Christians should not be obsessing about babysitting high-maintenance believers. They should be looking at the fields.

The compromised will tell you that your call to win souls is divisive. But to postpone soul winning for the sake of human unity is the most divisive thing you can do. Run to the harvest and dump the lukewarm spectators.

4. By staying back, you choose lukewarm Christians over your children and grandchildren.

We have said a lot about our children, but we must! I hope it doesn't take this, but when your daughter comes home devastated by what she saw in the high school showers, maybe then you'll start fighting.

The Left is after your child. Nothing but revival and direct action will stop them. And when you stay out of politics, out of deference to tepid do-nothings, you are choosing them over your child and grandchild.

If you are not taking action against the moral threats coming against your family because you don't want to rock the boat at your church, *be warned*! The Bible has a severe opinion.

First Timothy 5:8: "But if anyone does not provide for his own, and especially for those of his household, he has denied the faith and is worse than an unbeliever."

5. The Bible tells you to turn away from lukewarm Christians.

Second Timothy 3:5 (AMPC) says, "For [although] they hold a form of piety (true religion), they deny and reject and are strangers to the power of it [their conduct belies the genuineness of their profession]. Avoid [all] such people [turn away from them]."

Now ask yourself, "Why does the Bible tell me to get away from them?" It is dangerous to hang out with them. They are draining, distracting, and disabling you from entering revival and reformation.

You also need to get away because you are different. Remember the misfits in chapter 8? I think that's you. You are one of those Jesus followers who love just a little too much—who want more than everyone thinks is right.

Maybe the lukewarm ones roll their eyes when you talk about awesome things you believe God can still do in this dark and evil time. They tell you your agitation is abnormal. They tell you to relax, but that just stokes your inner fire. They tell you, "God is in control, and you don't have to worry."

But you remember the Word of God, and it tells you to do something. You know that God combs the earth for willing vessels who will throw off the glad rags of religion, take up the mighty weapons of God, and thrust the sword of the Spirit into the heart of the powers of darkness.

Chapter 13

A PARENTS' GUIDE TO PROTECTING YOUR CHILD AGAINST WOKE SCHOOLS

By Christie Verarde

Author's note: I have asked my dear friend Christie Verarde to write this chapter. Christie has a master's degree in human growth and development and forty-five years' experience in the early childhood field as both a preschool teacher and a college instructor. Most of all, she is a very powerful woman of God.

WHILE WE HAVEN'T been looking, something dangerous has befallen our children. It imperils both their future and ours. As if lockdown and vaccine controversies weren't enough to contend with, a dramatic shift has occurred in their social world. In classrooms and on social media everywhere, children are being radicalized. They're being pressured to challenge established norms of identity, race, history, and gender. Nowhere is this radicalization more evident than in children's development. Traditional notions of what is developmentally appropriate for children have been overturned. Established scientific theory has been tossed aside.

This didn't happen suddenly; it has been emerging steadily for years, even decades. It can be seen in

- the increasingly sexualized toys marketed to our youngest, most impressionable kids—overly made-up dolls with exaggerated figures wearing super mini-skirts and see-through outfits;

- the undeveloped feet of young girls squeezed into adult-styled platforms and heeled shoes;

- drag queen story hours in public libraries across the country billed as educational and promoting healthy attitudes toward sexuality and gender fluidity; and

- a recent Pride event featuring a very minimally clad stripper who was pole dancing while holding a toddler up against her almost totally exposed breasts.[1]

Should we be surprised to see a wide variety of genders and behaviors being promoted in children's classrooms across the country? According to professor Carl Trueman, it's part of a larger collective shift in our perception of who we are. The self has been sexualized and politicized.

Not only has the self been sexualized, but the sexual self has been severed from biology (more on that later). This newly minted sexual self is being advocated by our state schools to ever younger children. AMAZEworks is a curriculum guide for teachers promoting gender diversity and identity discussions in the classroom. It is used with children as young as three. Teachers share stories of "victimized" children like Ben, who likes to paint his fingernails. They follow up with questions designed to evoke shame in anyone who doesn't feel empathy for Ben's victim status. Students are encouraged to think that cross-gender curiosity shows that they secretly want to be something other than what they are biologically.

A friend of mine taught preschool for close to thirty years. During that period, she cared for several boys who came to class with painted nails. None of the other children made fun of them, and more importantly, none of those boys grew up to be gay men. The fact is that cross-gender play is a normal part of play and learning. Children try on different roles to learn about themselves and the world around them. To assert that cross-gender play indicates a child's divergent gender preference and secret cry for its recognition is seriously misguided and harmful. By casting children who cross-gender-play as victims of a repressive culture, teachers encourage them to adopt an artificial victim status to benefit from whatever empowerment and sense of belonging it provides. They implicitly teach children that expressing themselves individually and sexually supersedes *all* other factors and concerns, including biology, nature, family, society, and religion—and that doing so is liberating and revolutionary.

At one time not long ago gender development theory was grounded on a solid scientific base. If you looked up that topic in a college textbook, you would invariably find the work of Lawrence Kohlberg and his influencer, Jean Piaget. Kohlberg's work has been the standard for understanding children's gender development for more than fifty years. His theory includes the following stages of development:

1. **Gender identity** appears around two years of age and continues until the child is around three years, six months. During this developmental stage a child recognizes that he or she is a boy or a girl based on physical characteristics.

2. **Gender stability** appears around three years, six months, and continues to around five years. During this stage a child learns that their gender is fixed for life. They state that as a girl, they will grow up to be like mommy; if a boy, they will grow up to be like

daddy. It means they understand as they age that they will remain their biological sex.

3. **Gender constancy** begins at around five to seven years, during which the child learns that their gender is constant despite any changes in behavior or appearance, meaning they can put on clothing or be involved in activities typically connected to the opposite sex and remain who they are.

Kohlberg's work is now being challenged and deemed passé. Today's teachers encourage children to "stay open" to their gender identity. It is no longer considered a constant. Instead, it is believed to be fluid and changeable throughout one's lifetime. Following is one of the current models taught to young educators in institutes of higher learning today.

Stage 1—a child experiences "Foreclosed Cisgender Identity"

Stage 2—a child can develop along three varying developmental experiences: Gender Moratorium, Gender Diffusion, or Commitment to Gender Identity

Stage 3—a child begins the "Development of the Identity"

Stage 4—a child begins their "Social and Political Awareness" of living in their chosen identity[2]

It is well documented in multiple scientific studies that children learn best when interacting with pattern and repetition. To create confusion and disallow children to see the simple genetic patterned development of men and women is not only misguided and unscientific—considering what we know about the developing brain—but it is unkind and self-serving. Could it be that those who advocate gender fluidity in children are doing so in hopes that a greater swath of society will come to view the aberrant as normal?

As attentive Christian parents, how do we confront these changes and protect our children? It is imperative to be clear about the beliefs you seek to preserve, how far you are willing to go to protect them, and your role in that scenario.

Let's discuss the parents' role in their child's care and learning. What is a parent? The *Oxford American Dictionary* defines a parent as "a father or mother."[3] *Merriam-Webster* defines a parent as "one that begets or brings forth offspring."[4] Another definition of *parent* refers to the primary adult caregiver that looks after the child's basic needs, such as feeding and safety. This includes relatives who have taken on the responsibility of child-rearing from biological parents for whatever reason, such as grandparents, older siblings, uncles, aunts, family friends, and step- or foster parents. What they all have in common is that they are responsible for that child's upbringing, which includes meeting their social, emotional, and physical needs.

The bond between a child and their primary caregiver is, and should be, very strong. Attachment is a crucial need for a child. Many scientific studies, such as the work of Patricia Kuhl at the University of Washington, show that children learn through relationships.

Who is not a parent? Governmental agencies and school boards. Primary caregivers should not be disrespected in their roles by societal or educational entities that feel they can "parent" a child better than the primary caregiver.

Currently, the idea of collective parenting is popular, and the traditional practice of private parenting is being attacked. Melissa Harris-Perry, a columnist and commentator, and the host of morning radio news program *The Takeaway*, has essentially said that schools should move into more of a parenting role. She believes we need to break the idea of private parenting, the notion that children belong to parents. Instead, she states that children belong to whole communities. In contrast, Scripture and the church lay the task of parenting squarely on the shoulders of those directly in the child's life.

The following guide, I believe, will be helpful to parents who want to address Woke culture being pushed on their children.

How God Views Your Position as a Parent

As Christians we find life in the Scriptures. We look to the Bible to help us navigate the world. Thinking about how to parent and who we are as parents is no exception. Here are a few choice verses that lay out how God sees our role:

Parents are to recognize their child's value.

- Psalm 127:3: "Behold, children are a heritage from the LORD, the fruit of the womb is a reward."

We are to love them.

- Psalm 103:13: "As a father pities his children, so the LORD pities those who fear Him."

- Colossians 3:21: "Fathers, do not provoke your children, lest they become discouraged."

- 1 Peter 5:2–3: "Shepherd the flock of God which is among you, serving as overseers, not by compulsion but willingly, not for dishonest gain but eagerly; nor as being lords over those entrusted to you, but being examples to the flock."

- Proverbs 31:26–28: "She opens her mouth with wisdom, and on her tongue is the law of kindness. She watches over the ways of her household, and does not eat the bread of idleness. Her children rise up and call her blessed; her husband also, and he praises her."

Parents are to teach them the Word of God.

- Deuteronomy 11:18–19: "Therefore you shall lay up these words of mine in your heart and in your soul, and bind them as a sign on your hand, and they shall be as frontlets between your eyes. You shall teach them to your children, speaking of them when you sit in your house, when you walk by the way, when you lie down, and when you rise up."

- Proverbs 22:6: "Train up a child in the way he should go, and when he is old he will not depart from it."

We are to discipline them as God disciplines us.

- Hebrews 12:10–11: "For they indeed for a few days chastened us as seemed best to them, but He for our profit, that we may be partakers of His holiness. Now no chastening seems to be joyful for the present, but painful; nevertheless, afterward it yields the peaceable fruit of righteousness to those who have been trained by it."

Nowhere in Scripture does it state that the community shall teach children the Word of God or that the community shall discipline one's children. That responsibility lies squarely on the shoulders of the adults parenting the child. Caring for a child's needs, including their education, is the job of primary caretakers, not the community.

FIVE STEPS TO FIGHTING BACK

The time has long passed when parents can comfortably assume their neighborhood school is raising their children in a manner consistent with Christian values. It is time to protect what we know to be right for our children. Here are five steps parents can take to stand against the influence of Woke culture in the classroom.

1. Know the issues you want to address in schools and society.

It is important to read up on the subjects you are concerned about and want to see changed in society. Find out what's happening in the news related to children's learning. Find and read authors on the subjects that relate to children. The internet is full of information that relates to children and their education. Talk with other like-minded parents. Talk with children about what they hear in their classrooms. Meet the children and families who are part of your child's social structure and hopefully meet allies in the fight.

Once you are ready to move forward, what issues should you address? Woke culture has its tentacles in several classroom areas, but three of the most serious areas are pronoun usage in the classroom, critical race theory, and gender development and identity. It would be overwhelming and frankly ineffective to address all these areas in a single protest. What specifically do you want to address? Which topic are you best suited to confront? Narrowing your protest will make it easier to construct your points cohesively. Your audience will be more open to one area of conflict and won't feel as if they are attacked from every side. In other words, release your protests over time. Slow and steady wins the race.

2. Know the channel of authority and the best office to bring your request/opposition to.

If you feel your child's rights have been violated and you want to bring a complaint to their school or district, start with their teacher. Perhaps there was a misunderstanding between your child and the classroom instructor. Clearing it up at that level would be the best scenario. If that doesn't work, move up the ladder of command to the local principal. If you don't find resolution there, your next stop would be at the district office with the school superintendent. If the teacher made an egregious error, you could always file a disciplinary report with the state agency that certifies teachers in your area.

3. Know your rights and be prepared to fight.

You can, and should, contend against the Woke indoctrination of your children in their educational institutions, but how? In a recent Fox News article, Ian Prior, a senior adviser at America First Legal and executive director of fightforschools.com, laid out some important information parents can use to discover exactly what is being taught at their children's school. He suggests "attending school board meetings, writing letters to the editor [of your local paper], and continuing to grow the ranks of watchdog moms and dads."[5]

Prior also mentions the Protection of Pupil Rights Amendment (PPRA). This legal tool gives parents the right to review any instructional materials used by the school, including all curriculum and teacher training. And best of all, the use of PPRA is free. If you visit aflegal.org, you will find a sample letter in its resources area. This letter can be used to submit a request to peruse curriculum and other instructional documents. Some districts may not want to hand the information over and may claim "copyright issues" as the reason. Following is a recent statement from the website of Ian Prior related to a current case with the West Perry School District of Pennsylvania: "Parents seeking accountability from their school systems are continually being told by school bureaucrats that providing them with instructional materials would 'violate copyright law.' That is a bogus claim, has no support in the law."[6]

In the Fox article, Prior further states that the PPRA prohibits schools from surveying your children about their family life, religion, political beliefs, or sex without offering parents an opportunity for their children to opt out of those conversations.

Prior's Fox News article concludes by describing the Freedom of Information Act (FOIA) as "one of the most powerful tools in the arsenal of a watchdog mom or dad." This tool can give you information about how the curriculum you requested with your PPRA is implemented, who approved it, and the funds used to purchase it. Most school districts are set up to offer this option online, but be specific about your requests. They may push back and charge you fees or hold back information as unattainable if the request is too broad.[7]

4. Pray up and know your support system.

When I look at young children, I am amazed. Few things are more adorable than watching a child view the world and try to take it all in. Alison Gopnik, a professor of psychology and affiliate professor of philosophy at UC Berkeley, likens children's curious brains to a lantern because their focus and concentration are on multiple things at the same time. They are excited by and interested in everything, which makes them vulnerable. They depend on us to create healthy, safe environments and filter out harmful information. That is a massive responsibility, but declaring our commitment to protect children is a God-given responsibility.

Considering the craziness being pushed on children from so many directions, the task of protecting them seems overwhelming. We are not alone. We need to pray for guidance and ask the Holy Spirit to intervene. The time for thinking about change has passed. We need to rise as an army of protective saints who hold the value of children to be sacred. To successfully counter this harm to our children, we must be prepared in the Word and prayed up in the Spirit. We will rise in His strength to meet the challenges we face. Let us become what today's children need us to be on their behalf—warriors of truth and godly love. "If two of you agree on earth concerning anything that they ask, it will be done for them by my Father in heaven" (Matt. 18:19).

As we may become fatigued during the fight, it is important to build a support system in advance. This could be family, neighbors, or like-minded parents. These are all good; however, the most important support system may well be found in your local church. Talk to your pastor. Is the congregation aware of the issues at your school and in your community? Do they pray about these issues and offer to stand with you in the fight? Hopefully, the answer is yes. If not, maybe it's time to find another church—one that will properly support you as you work to protect your children.

5. Follow up and be diligent.

The work of protecting children in this society is not an easy one. It will take your time and your consistent effort and may require financial adjustment on your part as well. Some parents are taking a hard look at their incomes and deciding to cut back so they can homeschool their children instead of sending them to public schools, where they might not be able to control what their children learn. Other parents are choosing to place their children in private schools, if feasible. But even that is not a solution if the private school follows a Woke agenda. Catholic and Evangelical school enrollments are exploding for that reason.

There is no one-size-fits-all way to approach this. Each family must make decisions about their children's education based on how they believe God wants them to parent and how God is leading them. Whatever path you take—public school, private school, or homeschooling—being involved in what your children learn is a privilege and a blessing. Stay the course. You will be rewarded.

In closing, we all know the song "Jesus Loves Me, This I Know."

> Jesus loves me, this I know,
> for the Bible tells me so.
> Little ones to Him belong;
> they are weak, but he is strong.
> Yes, Jesus loves me!
> Yes, Jesus loves me!
> Yes, Jesus loves me!

The Bible tells me so.[8]

It's such a simple song, yet it has such a strong message. Little ones to Him *do* belong, and we can partner with Him in protecting them. Jesus exhorts us, "Let the little children come to Me, and do not forbid them; for of such is the kingdom of heaven" (Matt. 19:14).

Thank You, dear God, for giving us charge over Your little ones. May we accept and carry out our duties with the help of Your unfailing grace. Amen.

Chapter 14

THE BURNING QUESTION: HOW WILL WE WIN ALL THESE SOULS?

W E HAVE COME to the burning question of this book. Let's take a moment to consider the meaning of the idiom "a burning question." Its meaning is a question that needs to be answered in the same way a house fire needs to be put out.

The fire we need to put out is this: How will we win all these lost souls?

This book has revealed three ongoing phenomena:

1. Vast fields of human souls are ripening all around us.

2. An American public that to all the world looks to be running from God is actually moving in His direction.

3. The things we deem to be obstacles to soul winning have instead created the climate for a mass harvest.

If these phenomena are true—and I know they are—then I repeat the burning question: How will we win all these souls? And this question breaks down into many smaller but equally important questions, such as: What is our message to America? What methods should we employ to ensure we do not lose this harvest?

The answer to all these questions begins with the phrase "The Lord of the harvest." Here are the verses where Christ first introduces this phrase:

> Then Jesus went about all the cities and villages, teaching in their synagogues, preaching the gospel of the kingdom, and healing every sickness and every disease among the people. But when He saw the multitudes, He was moved with compassion for them, because they were weary and scattered, like sheep having no shepherd. Then He said to His disciples, "The harvest truly is plentiful, but the laborers are few. Therefore, pray the Lord of the harvest to send out laborers into His harvest."
>
> —MATTHEW 9:35–38

Jesus is telling them to pray to God the Father—the Lord of the harvest. God the Father is the Who, what, where, and when of soul winning.

MY STORY

Let me tell you the shocking story of how I found this out. I was twenty years old, preaching in a small church. The passion for winning the lost consumed me. Night after night I left that little church devastated that no one was getting saved.

I could not stand it any longer. The lack of souls was wrecking me emotionally and making me physically sick. Then I made a foolish vow to God. I told Him I would quit the ministry if no souls were born again in my next meeting.

That night it seemed as if the entire world were against me. On the one night I needed the most help, thunder, lightning, and hard rain thinned the crowd. I preached my heart out but to no avail. No one was saved. It all felt like an emphatic statement.

I was staying at a Christian resort a few miles from the little church. The drive back became treacherous as the downpour flooded the dark country road I was on. I was crying and emotionally wrecked as I faced the prospect of leaving the ministry. I was in no condition to drive.

I had one small bridge left to cross, and the rising creek was attacking it. When I finally arrived at my hotel, in my emotional state, reaching safety provided no relief. I parked, grabbed my Bible and some preaching notes I never wanted to see again, and got soaked running to the lobby. It was the perfect storm.

Once in my room, I began to pace. I did not know how to pray in this situation—or even if I should. It was 10:30 p.m. Midnight would make it official. I would be out of the ministry.

My anxiety kept mounting, only to be outdone by my disappointment. The inner fire to win the lost is hard to gain and even harder to quench. Watching the minutes pass, I felt like a prisoner on death row, awaiting execution and hoping for that call from the governor granting a stay.

Ironically, the phone in my room did ring an hour later, at around 11:30. But it was no reprieve; instead, it was like rubbing salt in my wounds. The voice on the other end was the last person I ever expected to hear from.

"Hi, Mario. It's Bob."

It was an atheist classmate from my high school. He had the locker next to mine and made it a point to torment me every day.

I replied, "How did you get this number, and what do you want?"

Of course, I knew exactly what he wanted and precisely how he got my number—I was sure Satan had given him my number and provoked him to call at just the right moment to put the finishing touches of humiliation on me. But what he said next was nothing at all like what I expected.

"Mario, I didn't call you to say hello. I just found out you are staying at this resort. I became a Christian after high school." Let me interject here and say that if Bob could get saved, anyone can get saved!

He continued, "I also didn't call you to tell you I am a Christian. I'm calling you because I'm a chaplain with the California Youth Authority. We are doing a conference here. We do a late-night devotional for young gang members and drug addicts. Our guest speaker didn't make it because the bridge washed out. Can you come and speak to them tonight?"

Have you ever seen a cartoon where someone is on the phone and suddenly the person they are talking to is standing right there? Yeah, it was like that. In a moment, he was standing next to me outside my hotel room door, and I said, "Where are they? I haven't got much time."

That very night, not a single one of those youth escaped salvation. Before the clock struck twelve, they were safely in the kingdom of God.

I found my harvest. Now let's find yours.

God's greatest protection might be when He prevents us from becoming skilled at something we are not supposed to do. I did not belong with the church crowd. Jesus loves the church, and some are indeed called to congregations. But I belonged in the harvest. And God the Father, in answer to my cry and in His mercy, put me there.

ALL THE PRINCIPLES IN MY TESTIMONY ARE ALSO IN THIS BOOK

- The very things I believed were ending my ministry were starting it. Even the bridge that was such a threat was part of God's plan. If the bridge had not washed out, my opportunity to preach would have been lost. In the same way, our national storm will serve the very same purpose.

- Only God! God had Elijah pour water on the sacrifice on Mount Carmel to remove all doubt that it was God who answered by fire. In the same way, the lack of souls, the rain—the entire ordeal—only served to place an exclamation point on the miracle. I could never claim any credit for the results of my ministry.

- I had to find my crowd. God the Father knows where the fields are and how to get you to those fields. You need not languish with people who don't want to receive.

- The frustration during the time of isolation pulled the bowstring so far back that it launched me into a lifetime of soul winning.

- How we will win souls starts with seeing God the Father's viewpoint on soul winning. He will look elsewhere for help to bring in the harvest if we do not see it.

But let's dig deeper. The greatest threat to soul winning is not outside the church but inside the church. If ever a barking dog slowed the soul-winning train, it was this one: an *anti*-soul-winning attitude. We can use all the excuses we want, but the truth is that we are about to lose America because we stopped winning souls.

SEEING SOULS THE WAY GOD DOES

The miracle harvest that awaits you begins with a sobering truth. We are at odds with God the Father regarding soul winning. He sees winning the lost as the supreme function of the church.

God the Father gave His Son for one major reason. It's found in John 3:16: "For God so loved the world that He gave His only begotten Son, that whoever believes in Him should not perish but have everlasting life." Sometimes the most important truths are so simple and familiar that we lose the meaning entirely.

So let's rehearse this with a quick question-and-answer session.

- How much did God the Father love the world? So much that He gave His only Son. That is what He did.

- Why did He give His Son? So that souls would not be
  lost.

You and I can name all sorts of things we think the church should be doing. But we are on totally different frequencies when we do not win souls. And the fact of the matter is, we simply don't see the supremacy of winning souls the way God the Father does.

Soul winning is not primarily attacked in the church by direct words, although sometimes it is. It is usually attacked by culture and attitude. Many Christian leaders bristle when I say this, but it is true. I can cite simple examples:

- Many Christian meetings end with no appeal for lost
  souls to be saved.

- Christians are not being trained to witness or to
  bring their friends to church.

- Even when there is an appeal to come to Christ, it is
  a nervous plea tacked on to the service.

- Instead of a towering gospel presentation, it is presented in fits and spurts. The outsider is surprised
  when the preacher suddenly switches gears in an "oh
  by the way" altar call.

But the real culprit is the selfish congregation. If the average pastor were to announce and give a total gospel message that laid out the work of the cross, the threat of hell, and the promise of the return of Christ, he would be attacked by members who complained that "such a simple message did not feed them."

To win souls, you must detach yourself from all anti-soul-winning Christian groups. If you don't, when the next call comes for the impending harvest, being around these people will deafen you to the voice of God.

The sleepy church will not stop God from finding workers, but it will embarrass the leaders of these lukewarm congregations. Many Christian leaders who have served God for years will become jealous of nobodies that emerge from nowhere and win thousands, perhaps millions, to Christ.

Tragically, these leaders will likely ignore the obvious reason for being skipped over. They will simply think it is unfair and therefore not legitimate. All they must do to enjoy the harvest is repent and jump in.

Now We Must Talk About Prayer

The immediate command of Jesus was "pray [to] the Lord of the harvest" (Luke 10:2). Interestingly, we do not see where Jesus taught His disciples how to preach. But He did teach them to pray.

What must prayer consist of if even preaching does not rank as its equal? I am not saying preaching is not important. I am saying that a sermon will ignite a thousandfold more from prayer than from the mechanics of public speaking.

What are we praying? Notice this: our prayer must be the urgent reaction to finding out souls are ready to be saved, and we must have workers to go and get them before it is too late.

Jesus is not saying we should pray for lost souls to get ready or to make them responsive to the preaching. We are imploring the Father to send workers before the harvest is lost. Why are we imploring God the Father about this? Because He has the power to send.

As you survey America, God needs to open your eyes. Jesus said, "Look to the fields!" It is possible not to see the forest for the trees. Our minds and hearts might be so weighed down with "facts" about what Americans want that we cannot see what they really want—and who it is that wants it.

Prayer will lift you out of limits and evil. It will cleanse you of the world's noise and clamor. Satan controls the soundtrack and the volume—until you pray.

But a part of this call to prayer is almost like a trick. God knows that you cannot sincerely pray for workers to be sent into the harvest without it causing their hearts to want to be sent.

> Then one of the seraphim flew to me, having in his hand a live coal which he had taken with the tongs from the altar. And he touched my mouth with it, and said: "Behold, this has touched your lips; your iniquity is taken away, and your sin purged."
>
> Also, I heard the voice of the Lord, saying: "Whom shall I send, and who will go for Us?"
>
> Then I said, "Here am I! Send me."
>
> —ISAIAH 6:6–8

WHAT IS A HARVEST?

Now we come to a critical insight. Let me ask you a question. What is a harvest? Think before you answer. You will soon see that it is much more than meets the eye.

You can say that a harvest is an event. It is a specific happening. This means it lasts for a certain amount of time—what a farmer calls harvesttime. But it is much more than that.

Harvest is an act of bringing in the crop. Therefore, it is also a master plan. So that there is no loss due to a labor shortage, a harvester must know not only when to harvest but also how big the harvest is likely to be.

A harvest is a master plan in the sense that the farmer must know what fields to harvest and when. This means they have a supreme sense of the condition of the crop, when it was planted, and which field is ready now.

This gives us another name for God the Father: the master planner of the harvest. He has been working in the fields. To harvest those fields, God sent His Son.

Then His Son sent us the Holy Spirit. He was not a parting gift to comfort the disciples for the loss of Jesus' physical presence. He is the supreme general of earth operations for the body of Christ!

Let's not stop here. Let's look at the big picture. Long before you and I were aware of the harvest, the Holy Spirit was working on hearts.

We know these verses, but we need to see them in a broader light.

> Nevertheless I tell you the truth. It is to your advantage that I go away; for if I do not go away, the Helper will not come to you; but if I depart, I will send Him to you. And when He has come, He will convict the world of sin, and of righteousness, and of judgment: of sin, because they do not believe in Me; of righteousness, because I go to My Father and you see Me no more; of judgment, because the ruler of this world is judged.
> —John 16:7–11

Like I said in the opening of this book, the work of the Holy Spirit is to envelop the earth with the conviction of sin, righteousness, and judgment. Missionaries working in tribes that had never seen anyone from the outside world have been amazed at the Holy Spirit's work when the tribesmen told them they had received warnings that someone was coming to bring them the truth.

This is happening in America. The Holy Spirit is working on hearts. It is a deep work.

It's Time to Cease From Your Labor

Now comes the most important thing you must know about the harvest. The church is weak and divided because God is doing something among the people, and the church is doing something totally independent of that. To bring in the harvest, we must quit doing things our way and surrender to the ongoing master plan of God's harvest.

Think about it. The prayer Jesus prescribed was this: "The harvest truly is plentiful, but the laborers are few. Therefore pray the Lord of the harvest to send out laborers into His harvest" (Matt. 9:37–38).

These laborers were somewhere else and had to be called into the harvest. So where were they? And what were they doing?

If you are truly open to what I am trying to tell you, then you are ready to hear the next burning truth: you cannot do His labor until you cease from your own. This means you are waking up to the reality that you have been working *for* God, not *with* Him.

Now we are to lay it all down and only take up what we are instructed to do. And those instructions can be very exotic!

When California was locked down during the pandemic, the state closed five of our tent crusades overnight. There was nothing we could do—or so I thought. I prayed because I felt utterly devastated not to be winning souls. Little did I know I was about to cease from my labors and be placed in the center of the harvest of God's kingdom.

It began when I became aware of the teachings of Jesus in Matthew 7:7–11:

> Ask, and it will be given to you; seek, and you will find; knock, and it will be opened to you. For everyone who asks receives, and he who seeks finds, and to him who knocks it will be opened. Or what man is there among you who, if his son asks for bread, will give him a stone? Or if he asks for a fish, will he give him a serpent? If you then, being evil, know how to give good gifts to your children, how much more will your Father who is in heaven give good things to those who ask Him!

I didn't realize the amazing thing going on in that chapter. A leper at the foot of the mountain was listening to these words, and it gave him the audacity to break Jewish Law and ask Jesus for healing. He heard Jesus say something that made him realize he was a child of God who could ask and receive.

But it would only appear to violate the Law until his miracle vindicated everything.

> When He had come down from the mountain, great multitudes followed Him. And behold, a leper came and worshiped Him, saying, "Lord, if You are willing, You can make me clean." Then Jesus put out His hand and touched him, saying, "I am willing; be cleansed." Immediately his leprosy was cleansed. And Jesus said to him, "See that you tell no one; but go your way, show yourself to the priest, and offer the gift that Moses commanded, as a testimony to them."
> —MATTHEW 8:1–4

For the moment, Jesus too appeared to break Jewish social-distancing laws about lepers, but again, it was vindicated. Why was I studying this? Because it was about to change my life forever.

That night in the middle of the night, I saw the face of a man. The vision startled me awake. His face was the most pitiful and tortured face I have ever seen. He was a composite of every miserable thing suffered by the homeless and the addicts along Highway 99 in California. He said to me in this vision: "If you want to, you can help me."

When I woke up, I realized that like Jesus and the leper, I could only help the man in my dream by breaking the law. I called our tent crusade leaders and told them, "We are going to Fresno to do a tent crusade in the middle of a lockdown." They got all excited, but it would have been a moot point if we could not find a tent site.

But why would God send the vision if we could not? You see, now I was operating with the Lord of the harvest. Now I was a part of a multifaceted act of God.

We found a large, beautiful park in Fresno that was independently owned. We point-blank asked the owners if they would let us do a full-blown tent crusade in the middle of a lockdown. We made it clear: "It could get us all arrested, and all of you could lose your business license."

Honestly, I felt sure they would say no, and then I would be off the hook. But they said, "Yes! We are sick of this lockdown and want to oppose it." What do you think happened next? We did a crusade, and not a single person got COVID-19.

Thousands came from everywhere to be saved and healed. The whole city knew about us. We had coffee with the mayor. He had tears in his eyes when he heard of the masses being saved and healed. Later, in the fullness of time, the Supreme Court agreed that the lockdowns were illegal. But by God's Spirit, we had known it all along.

Can you see what I am telling you? God the Father has a master plan for your harvest of souls. Pray until you are dead to human planning and alive only to go forth at His command. Heaven will back you up.

Yes, your instructions will be strange and wonderful. But they will take you to the greatest experience of your life—a mass harvest of souls!

Chapter 15

YOU ARE A DESTROYER
OF THE DEVIL'S WORKS

I N THIS CHAPTER you will learn the explosive truth that your assignment in the army of God is your individual expression and extension of Christ's destruction of the works of the devil. You are a destroyer of the devil's works. God will give you a way to do it that is unique to you.

Until that gets through to you—until you admit and agree to those terms—God will remain silent about your assignment. Because the situation today in America is an impossible one, only one kind of person will make a difference now. They must be armed with divine certainty. They must own an unshakable, bone-deep conviction that they have been chosen for this task. To understand this, I must first take you back to the Garden of Eden.

It was a horrible day for you and me when Adam and Eve lost their lives in the Garden of Eden. It is impossible to measure what they lost and the curse we gained.

Remember what God had in mind for us: "Let Us make man in Our image, according to Our likeness; let them have dominion over the fish of the sea, over the birds of the air, and over the cattle, over all the earth and over every creeping thing that creeps on the earth" (Gen. 1:26).

They gave up their royalty and embraced slavery, bondage to sin, and life on Satan's terms. Why did they take a bite of evil? The devil presented them with an alternate reality. And the devil doesn't do it just once but over and over in history. There is a lot to see in what Satan said to Eve.

> Now the serpent was more cunning than any beast of the field which the LORD God had made. And he said to the woman, "Has God indeed said, 'You shall not eat of every tree of the garden'?"
>
> And the woman said to the serpent, "We may eat the fruit of the trees of the garden; but of the fruit of the tree which is in the midst of the garden, God has said, 'You shall not eat it, nor shall you touch it, lest you die.'"
>
> Then the serpent said to the woman, "You will not surely die. For God knows that in the day you eat of it your eyes will be opened, and you will be like God, knowing good and evil."
>
> So, when the woman saw that the tree was good for food, that it was pleasant to the eyes, and a tree desirable to make one wise, she took of its fruit and ate. She also gave to her husband with her, and he ate.
>
> —GENESIS 3:1–6

First, Satan tried to make her doubt what she heard. Did God really say that? When that didn't work, he called God a liar. "You will not die." Then he told her, "God said that because He is afraid you will also become a god."

Satan's words are a microcosm of every occult, witchcraft, New Age, and false religion in the world. Whether it is nirvana or becoming "Clear" through "thetan levels" in Scientology, or whether it deals directly with the devil for power, all of it is about casting off boundaries to become God.

Satan lies, saying, "Trust me. I will be your apprentice—until I overpower you and become the master." Bottom line: you only *think* you can bargain with the devil.

Now here comes the urgent part. Let's look again at Genesis 3:6 and add verse 7.

> So when the woman saw that the tree was good for food, that
> it was pleasant to the eyes, and a tree desirable to make one
> wise, she took of its fruit and ate. She also gave to her hus-
> band with her, and he ate. Then the eyes of both of them were
> opened, and they knew that they were naked; and they sewed
> fig leaves together and made themselves coverings.

It is fascinating that the Bible describes the moment humankind
went blind as "Then the eyes of both of them were opened." This
describes Wokeness perfectly: you go blind in the name of waking
up. Your new eyes see nothing but suspicion, shame, and evil.

Jesus also described this condition. "Your eye is like a lamp that
provides light for your body. When your eye is healthy, your whole
body is filled with light. But when it is unhealthy, your body is
filled with darkness. Make sure that the light you think you have is
not actually darkness" (Luke 11:34–35, NLT).

When life is seen through the Woke lens, everything that was
once beautiful is now ugly. No one can be trusted. Everyone is
phobic. Every day we must find more evil, worse words, and more
things that offend.

A terminal self-righteousness overtakes you. Believing in yourself is now a runaway obsession, and your "identity" takes prece-
dence over everything. You no longer believe in *the* truth. You only
believe in *your* truth. Nothing gets in your way—not science, facts,
reality, or God.

In Genesis, suddenly all Adam and Eve could see was shame
and fear. The same thing has happened to America. Overnight,
Wokeness seemed to be everywhere. Why is that? Just like Adam's
and Eve's change of sight in the Garden, the Woke way of seeing
things has a demonic origin.

Here is the point: The depravity, blatant hatred of God, and tyranny of our government are all part of the same demonic event.
Woke lies are merely the latest manifestation of Satan's lies to Eve.

In thinking they would be free, they became enslaved. In

thinking they would become strong, they became addicted. They trusted that the new boss would be better than the old boss.

They were going to make the world better. They were going up one level—to an intelligent, enlightened, new-and-improved breed of human. Instead, they became debased, weak, and paralyzed by fear. Teachers' unions, transgenderism, leftist socialism, you name it—they have all fallen for the oldest lie in the book.

But God did not leave Adam and Eve without hope. The first gospel sermon in the Bible appears right after man fell in Genesis 3:15: "And I will put enmity between you and the woman, and between your seed and her Seed; He shall bruise your head, and you shall bruise His heel."

The Seed of the woman is Christ—and He crushed Satan's head on the cross. That enmity (hatred) for Satan carries down to us. We all share in Jesus Christ's declaration of war on the devil. That makes every believer a spiritual soldier, regardless of what we think. There is no exemption from this invisible war.

When we survey the battlefield, it is easy to ask, "Where is everybody?" The answer is that the teaching of the modern church has perverted the true identity of believers on earth. Our nation has deteriorated because Christians do not invoke the authority of the cross on satanic activity. Modern preaching has stripped the body of Christ of her true identity.

There is so much preaching on "finding your purpose." But our purpose was never lost. It has been clearly stated in the Bible all along. It never needed to be found. It needed to be obeyed. Here is what I mean. Just ask the millions of American believers who shuttle in and out of church one simple question: Why did Christ come to earth? They will answer, "To die for our sins."

That response, while it contains truth, is woefully inadequate. Now ask the Bible that same question. It replies, "He who sins is of the devil, for the devil has sinned from the beginning. For this purpose the Son of God was manifested, that He might destroy the works of the devil" (1 John 3:8). Your purpose is His purpose. You are to continue His mission.

Dying for your sins is something Christ did *for* you. Destroying the works of the devil is something He does *through* you. Satan wants you to park at the first truth because the second one can destroy all his works.

But modern Christian fads do even more damage. They cause us to live in denial, away from the battlefield. Yet avoiding our true mission is unnatural and unhealthy for a born-again believer.

After a season of this compromised existence, depression and anxiety can set in. This leads to an even deeper dependency on "therapeutic" sermons—messages that tell us how blessed and privileged we are.

The more you indulge in your "blessed privilege," the more passive you become. Then you are poisoned by another condition: I call it the "everything is in God's hands" syndrome. The urgent voice of God calling for someone to rise in His name and confront the evil is drowned out by preaching that says God is too good and we are too blessed to be responsible for dealing with the evil of our time.

Even powerful Christians can lose sight of their calling to destroy the devil's works. We are about to read of how it happened to a great missionary. The story is found in the book *Born for Battle* by R. Arthur Mathews.

> J. O. Fraser, pioneer missionary to the Lisu tribe in Southwest China with the China Inland Mission, experienced how intense the wrestling with the powers of darkness can be before the "strong man" is finally forced to yield up his prey. Here is an account of his soul travail as told by Mrs. Howard Taylor in *Behind the Ranges*:
>
>> Strange uncertainty began to overshadow his inward life. All he had believed and rejoiced in became unreal, and even his prayers seemed to mock him as the answers

faded into nothingness....In his solitude, depression such as he had never known before closed down on him....Deeply were the foundations shaken in those days and nights of conflict, until Fraser realized that behind it all were "powers of darkness" seeking to overwhelm him. He dared to invade Satan's kingdom, undisputed for ages. At first, vengeance had fallen on the Lisu inquirers, an easy prey. Now, he himself was attacked—and it was war to the death, spiritually.

It was at this stage, when he was tempted to end everything, that a magazine came in the mail. Eagerly he read and reread every word until the truth of the Word of God gripped him and set him free. This is how he himself describes what went on in his heart during those days:

> What it showed me was that deliverance from the power of the evil one comes through definite resistance on the ground of the Cross. I am an engineer and believe in things working....The passive side of leaving everything to the Lord Jesus as our life, while blessedly true, was not all that was needed just then. Definite resistance on the ground of the Cross was what brought me light. For I had found that it worked....The cloud of depression dispersed. I found that I could really have victory in the spiritual realm whenever I wanted it. The Lord Himself resisted Satan orally: "Get thee behind me, Satan!" I, in humble dependence on Him, did the same. I talked to Satan at that time, using the promises of Scriptures as weapons. And they worked.[1]

The changes we need in the American church are violent—but we must change! A deep sleep has settled on the very army that must be wide awake. The work God must do in us is painful, but it is not nearly as painful as the disaster that awaits us if we fail to repent and take authority.

The explosive defiance of Christ was evident from the beginning of His public ministry. He opened the Book of Isaiah and read it out loud. He makes an open declaration: "Here is what I am here to do!"

> The Spirit of the LORD is upon Me, because He has anointed Me to preach the gospel to the poor; He has sent Me to heal the brokenhearted, to proclaim liberty to the captives and recovery of sight to the blind, to set at liberty those who are oppressed; to proclaim the acceptable year of the LORD.
> —LUKE 4:18–19

Everything on Jesus' hit list targets a work of Satan. He leaves no doubt where and how His power will be demonstrated.

Acts 10:38 proves that He made good on His promise and His threat: "How God anointed Jesus of Nazareth with the Holy Spirit and with power, who went about doing good and healing all who were oppressed by the devil, for God was with Him."

Is God with you and me? The one way to know is that we destroy the works of the devil.

It's our turn now! That is a wonderful battle cry. But it rings hollow if we don't take hold of the truth that we are destroyers of the devil's works. We dare not take our turn without power. We dare not tangle with the forces of evil that hold America hostage without a blazing anointing.

It's our turn now! Those words can become just a meaningless catchphrase in a sea of catchphrases. Again and again, we have had our emotions stirred and hopes raised, only to be disappointed.

So many movements in the church have been washed away like footprints in the sand. They were doomed from the beginning by faulty motives and half-hearted attempts. We cannot do that again!

And we also cannot turn away in dismay! The opportunity is too big. The stakes are too high. All the elements of awakening and reformation are coming together. And we do not know when they will ever line up this way again.

Despite all the times it has failed before, I know in my heart that this time is different. It is different because of what I see God doing. He is creating people who can turn the tide of wickedness. He doesn't care about your age or your education. He searches for someone who is travailing over the evil. He is looking for people who cannot live without power and purpose. They want to be in the fight—they want to be in the thick of it.

God is pulling you out of the damaged religious crowd into special intimacy with Him. You will not pray the same way you did before. E. M. Bounds said,

> To say prayers in a decent, delicate way is not heavy work. But to pray really, to pray till hell feels the ponderous stroke, to pray till the iron gates of difficulty are opened, till the mountains of obstacles are removed, till the mists are exhaled and the clouds are lifted, and the sunshine of a cloudless day brightens—this is hard work, but it is God's work, and man's best labor.[2]

Be careful. When you pray like that, you might accidentally ask God who you really are. He will tell you that you are a destroyer of the devil's works. He will tell you that He can make you into the spiritual weapon you never imagined you could be.

When we drop all else and open the door for God's kingdom to overtake our lives and plans, we immediately connect to unlimited power, wisdom, favor, and resources. We can answer anyone, implement plans with wisdom from beyond this world, and connect to the others who have been overtaken by the kingdom. This is how nationwide spiritual fires are set and the course of a culture is transformed.

Living deep within you—and ready to come out—is a courageous declaration of war on the godless ideologies destroying our nation. Soon it will come pouring out of you, along with an irrevocable decision—a decision to be in the middle of God's greatest act in history.

Chapter 16

THE TONGUE OF FIRE

W E NEED A tongue of fire! It is a desperately needed gift. Not only do I need a tongue of fire, but I need everyone who reads this to believe they can have a tongue of fire. The best description I can give you for this gift is found in Luke 21:15: "For I will give you a mouth and wisdom which all your adversaries will not be able to contradict or resist."

Evil is working in America more through the perversion of the spoken word than through any other means. By hijacking the meaning of words, the cultural villains of our nation are taking over our freedoms. For instance, "equity" programs are not at all equal; they punish a certain segment of society and deny them an education and jobs. "Inclusion" means exclusion when you are the demographic they want to exclude.

Antifa means anti-fascist. So of course they practice fascist violence.[1] They use the perversion of words to justify beating people. Here is my take on how they think: "Your opinion is wrong. Since it is wrong, it is also hate speech—because I hate it. And since your hate speech is so stressful that it feels like physical violence, I have the right to attack you physically."

Lisa Feldman Barrett wrote for the *New York Times*, "If words can cause stress, and if prolonged stress can cause physical harm, then it seems that speech—at least certain types of speech—can be a form of violence."[2]

Black Lives Matter takes it even further with its heinous catchphrase "White silence is violence." In essence, it is saying, "I am not beating you up and burning your house because of anything you said; it is what you didn't say. Your silence threw the first punch. I am acting in self-defense."

What is my point? All these groups are saying, "You are not allowed to have an opinion other than mine. If you do, I can attack you."

This happened in the Bible. We see where Stephen's words were treated as an act of violence.

> "You stiff-necked and uncircumcised in heart and ears! You always resist the Holy Spirit; as your fathers did, so do you. Which of the prophets did your fathers not persecute? And they killed those who foretold the coming of the Just One, of whom you now have become the betrayers and murderers, who have received the law by the direction of angels and have not kept it."
>
> When they heard these things they were cut to the heart, and they gnashed at him with their teeth. But he, being full of the Holy Spirit, gazed into heaven and saw the glory of God, and Jesus standing at the right hand of God, and said, "Look! I see the heavens opened and the Son of Man standing at the right hand of God!"
>
> Then they cried out with a loud voice, stopped their ears, and ran at him with one accord; and they cast him out of the city and stoned him. And the witnesses laid down their clothes at the feet of a young man named Saul. And they stoned Stephen as he was calling on God and saying, "Lord Jesus, receive my spirit." Then he knelt and cried out with a loud voice, "Lord, do not charge them with this sin." And when he had said this, he fell asleep.
>
> —ACTS 7:51–60

This same murderous spirit is operating in America.

The tongue of fire is a gift. The fire that fell on the altar when Elijah prayed can fall on you. I am counting on it! The web of deceit

Satan has spun over our nation cannot be cut with just normal words. My prayer is that you and others who read this book will be transformed into mouthpieces of truth—with words of authority and surgical keenness to pierce the lies killing our nation.

God needs voices in our world. As evil grows stronger and more sophisticated, the Holy Spirit wants to give chosen vessels a tongue of fire. Again and again, I have tried to impress on you that it is our turn now. That means communicating the greatest message of love and hope that mankind has ever heard. But the communication cannot stop there.

Since it is all about communication, as the chosen come to the throne of God and offer themselves willingly to confront the curse on America, they will receive the language, the authority, the precise words, and the opportunity to speak them.

But before you can receive the fire from heaven, you must have some down-to-earth instruction on what speaking against evil involves.

There are endless right ways to speak out against evil. A parent can challenge Woke school boards and administrators. A believer can answer the Holy Spirit's prompting to run for political office.

The lost art of civil discourse is the most common and effective means of pushing back against evil. You can dispel lies by talking with loved ones, friends, and those in your circle of influence.

The key is prayer and preparation. You must arm yourself with good information. It is sad but true that we are all journalists now. That means we must double-check sources and verify our facts.

Many preachers have embarrassed themselves. They stepped right out of a congregation's safe atmosphere and into the political arena's glare. They can get away with saying certain things before an adoring crowd but not when they enter a den of lions with messy and slipshod material. Proverbs 25:26 says, "A righteous man who falters before the wicked is like a murky spring and a polluted well."

Leftists can lie with impunity. The media is biased toward them. But Christians cannot misstate anything—not even by accident.

They will jump all over you. It is not fair, but that is the arena we are operating in right now.

But there is consolation in this if you realize you are not trying to win over your opponent—you are trying to win the audience.

Think about it. Those videos of brave moms confronting a school board did not win over the school board. In fact, the board dug in its heels. But the crowd cheered, and the video went viral.

The same is true of voices like Candace Owens, Ben Shapiro, Jordan Peterson, Charlie Kirk, and many others. If they are on campus, before Congress, on a panel, or on television, they rarely persuade the interviewer or Congress. Their impact comes from the millions who saw and heard their message.

You have great power for influence because you have the Holy Spirit.

When you know your information inside and out, you will have the secret edge of debate: the power to remain calm.

You can depend on angry leftists to have a meltdown and start screeching. It is common for them to lack substance and honest facts. They love to spout slogans. And they lie with impunity because the media is biased toward them.

Christians get bad advice—especially about information. We have become a generation of poorly informed Christians. The devil tricked us into thinking we were spiritual by not studying what was happening around us. It was not "spiritual" to read certain books and to be oblivious to our rights as parents and citizens.

I am a reader. I am always in a book. The Bible is by far the book I read the most. But I read other books—I read them selectively. The Holy Spirit incorporates what I have read into messages.

In Acts 17, Paul delivers a timeless gospel message to the intellectuals in Athens. From Mars Hill he shows the supremacy of Christ. But at a key moment in his message, he quotes a Greek poet to strengthen his case for the supremacy of Christ over idols.

> For in Him we live and move and have our being, as also some of your own poets have said, "For we are also His offspring." Therefore, since we are the offspring of God, we ought not to think that the Divine Nature is like gold or silver or stone, something shaped by art and man's devising.
>
> —Acts 17:28–29

How jolly and lovable the American church felt by staying out of every arena of influence but church. And only now does it dawn on us how much real estate we have lost.

The Left spent time learning about all the mundane things that bore us. They got permits and took the open positions at polling places. They got the grants and looked compassionate. They educated the poor, only to go to them for help.

We need to study! First, to lay a foundation and worldview from the Bible and then to add useful information. "Study and do your best to present yourself to God approved, a workman [tested by trial] who has no reason to be ashamed, accurately handling and skillfully teaching the word of truth" (2 Tim. 2:15, AMP).

How pathetic do we look when the church says that Satan stole America when, in case after case, the church gave it away. But the rest of the story is even worse.

The American church not only stayed out of many parts of American life—it did not even handle its own business. The church stopped winning souls and making disciples.

The long, sad story of modern American Christianity is one of false success, counterfeit goals, and a breathtaking abdication of its calling. How can we possibly be surprised by the moral morass coming for our children?

So let's do something about all this! Yes, we begin with mundane human practicality. We need to study and learn about parents' rights, political agendas, and the tactics of Woke. But after that, we need a supernatural gift: the tongue of fire!

Do not ask for the fire unless you understand what it will do to you.

After five years of mediocre results and enjoying access to royalty, Isaiah came to a yawning episode of uncertainty. It was the year that King Uzziah died. Uzziah and Isaiah were first cousins. Uzziah's death was not just an event of state. It was personal and profound. The prophet was overcome with a desperate need for direction.

Isaiah went to pray in the temple. Surely God would console one of His choice servants. It was just the opposite. God decided to terrify Isaiah. I believe it was to jolt him out of complacency and human concerns. He was to be taken from human fear to divine fear so that he might obtain a tongue of fire, take the word of God to his generation, and give the greatest descriptions of Jesus to be found in the Old Testament.

> In the year that King Uzziah died, I saw the Lord sitting on a throne, high and lifted up, and the train of His robe filled the temple. Above it stood seraphim; each one had six wings: with two he covered his face, with two he covered his feet, and with two he flew. And one cried to another and said: "Holy, holy, holy is the LORD of hosts; the whole earth is full of His glory!" And the posts of the door were shaken by the voice of him who cried out, and the house was filled with smoke.
>
> So I said: "Woe is me, for I am undone! Because I am a man of unclean lips, and I dwell in the midst of a people of unclean lips; for my eyes have seen the King, the LORD of hosts."
>
> Then one of the seraphim flew to me, having in his hand a live coal which he had taken with the tongs from the altar. And he touched my mouth with it, and said: "Behold, this has touched your lips; your iniquity is taken away, and your sin purged."
>
> Also I heard the voice of the Lord, saying: "Whom shall I send, and who will go for Us?"
>
> Then I said, "Here am I! Send me."
>
> —ISAIAH 6:1–8

Oh! What a tongue of fire God gave to Isaiah! He would no longer use it for inferior purposes. It would divide good and evil. It would plainly declare the word of God with not a hint of his own opinion.

The man who walked into the temple looked nothing like the man who walked out. Hell convulsed at his approach. Satan writhed in anguish as once again he had failed to keep the word of God from coming to the next generation.

Let me ask you something. Do you want a tongue of fire? Would you speak words of life, holiness, conviction, and the authority to destroy the works of Satan?

Do you know what I want for you? I want you to feel a sickness in the pit of your stomach when you are around believers who don't see why we are so worked up about what is happening to America. I want you to feel the overpowering urge to run from the presence of those who say there is nothing we can do about it.

Do you know what I want for you? I want you to see the almighty Lord God high and lifted up. I want a white-hot coal on your lips. I want a cry to erupt from your spirit. I want you never to recover from that cry!

"How do I receive a tongue of fire?" you ask. You ask, fully understanding the implications. Isaiah tells us more about this gift in Isaiah 50:4: "The Lord GOD has given me the tongue of the learned, that I should know how to speak a word in season to him who is weary. He awakens me morning by morning, He awakens my ear to hear as the learned."

Only God knows who is reading this right now. Only God knows where you will declare the truth. It is getting so close to being your turn! Whether it is at a school, a boardroom, a living room, a church, an arena, or a stadium, it is all the same to Jesus.

There is one thing I am certain of: God would never give you a tongue of fire without giving you the platform to speak His message. How futile are the Woke Left's plans before God's power. Yes, they ban us, censor our videos, and keep us out of colleges and halls of power. But the ban cannot stand!

Jesus said in Luke 21:12–13, "But before all these things, they will lay their hands on you and persecute you, delivering you up to the synagogues and prisons. You will be brought before kings and rulers for My name's sake. But it will turn out for you as an occasion for testimony." *It will turn!*

The apostle Paul knew our frustration because he experienced the tangled web of deceit that existed in his day. He also knew the power of the tongue of fire. He did not just believe in presenting the truth; he believed in the surpassing authority of the flaming tongue to destroy falsehoods and wicked agendas. (See 2 Corinthians 10:4–5.)

On a day so long ago,

- Noah said he would speak the word of God to a wicked world and build a massive boat during a drought;

- Moses heard the voice say, "Go to Egypt and tell Pharaoh to let My people go";

- David said that the Lord was his shepherd and would give him the power to rule Israel and conquer its enemies, even though he had no training for such a task;

- Daniel was torn from his family and exiled to a pagan nation, but he said he would speak the word of God to the king of Babylon; and

- Saul of Tarsus was killing Christians and imprisoning them when a light brighter than the sun created the apostle Paul, who wrote much of the New Testament.

The same voice they heard is speaking to you now. Are you going to tell the Lord you can't do it? Will you tell Him how tangled your life is? Will you ask to be excused for lack of talent?

They heard that voice calling them. Now you hear it. How will you answer?

It's your turn *now*.

Chapter 17

A SUPERNATURAL WEAPON FOR A SUPERNATURAL THREAT

THIS CHAPTER IS about healing miracles, and I must warn you: some things in this chapter will be painfully honest. You may read some things you are not ready to read.

Healing miracles are utterly essential for us to take our turn at winning America. They are too important for us to look the other way because of some of the abuses happening today. We must not tolerate fake miracles and emotionalism.

David Wilkerson said this about the damage done by those guilty of fake healings.

> Most Christians today cringe when they hear these words! Why? Because these words have been made an abomination by unscrupulous, power-hungry preachers and teachers! The great tragedy is that such perversions have caused many God-fearing pastors, evangelists, and laypeople to turn away from the truth of a fully preached gospel.[1]

I am not saying this because I feel superior to any of my brothers and sisters in the ministry. Quite the opposite. Everything in this chapter is born of blood, sweat, and tears.

THREE WAYS TO SPOT THE FAKES

Here are three signs that miracles are being faked:

1. If you are in a meeting where the crowd is whipped into a crescendo of emotion before anything happens, you should leave. The reason is clear. A crowd in a frenzy is more susceptible to manipulation by the speaker. Boisterous praise should never be used to induce a miracle. Miracles and healings should cause the high praises of God to resound.

2. If the minister picks someone out of the crowd and engages in tedious details about names, addresses, and other trivia, beware. I have seen the Holy Spirit give names and addresses, but it is never a long, drawn-out affair. Dragging it out only brings attention to the minister and not God.

   Ask yourself how they know these things. Did they ask you to fill out a prayer card beforehand? Did they ask for information online before the meeting? Even if you just announce on social media that you are coming to their meeting, they can get details about you from your profile.

3. The final sign of a fake is related to money. Do they tie healing to giving to their ministry or spend an inordinate amount of time begging for money? This is not easy for me to write. But again, the stakes are too high to allow fakes to operate.

I am harder on myself than anyone else. I am continually checking my heart on the issue of miracles. Because of that, the enemy can attack me before a meeting.

There is a question he tries to haunt me with every time, a question about healing miracles. Is it right to invite the public to come to a meeting to be healed? There is always agony for me in that question.

When you make the announcement, it raises hope for people in desperate situations. And people make great sacrifices—sometimes unimaginable—to sit in our tent and believe for a miracle.

Then the meeting begins and my agony is replaced with a glory that words cannot describe. I see the radiant faces of those who testify that Christ has healed their bodies. Then, after the tent crusade ends, we get their reports. They tell us about going to doctors and getting medical follow-ups for their healing claims.

THE DAY I ALMOST DIED

To help you understand the stringent standards I feel for signs and wonders, I must tell you a story. This is the story of how I was almost killed at age twenty-two on the Berkeley campus.

I can still recall that day as if it just happened. I was so terrified of witnessing that I was pacing and praying all day on a hillside above the campus of forty-four thousand students. I asked God, "How do I reach a generation of students bent on Marxist revolution?"

One voice within me argued, "You must study the great modern apologists of the faith and give an intellectual defense of the faith. Immerse yourself in the writings of Francis Schaeffer, C. S. Lewis, and G. K. Chesterton." The other voice said simply, "Not by might nor by power, but by My Spirit" (Zech. 4:6).

The answer came emphatically that night at about 11 p.m. I was sharing my intellect-based apologetic faith with a flower child in front of the Student Union building of UC Berkeley. I could not see the massive, angry radical stealing up behind me.

As this Goliath of an atheist grabbed me by the neck and began choking the life out of me, I realized the words of great Christian intellectuals were useless at that point. And I was sure that young campus radical did not understand why he felt a sudden rage against me.

But the powers of darkness did. They understood what was at stake. Miracle-based soul winning is a grave threat to Satan, and demons will stop at nothing to kill a miracle ministry before it is born.

God ordered me to take my stand in the power of the Spirit, and in my own faltering way I did. My assailant suddenly stopped and stood still, stunned by something he saw behind me in the shadows. To this day I don't know what startled him; I only know that he released his grip on my throat, and I ran. I affirmed my commitment to the supernatural gospel of Christ as I ran.

That did it! Having settled the question, we began telling people they could come and be healed. We announced our first healing rally at Berkeley.

I was such a raw recruit that the night of the rally I stood in front of the audience, frozen in fear. In the crowd a young man lay unconscious on a couch at the back of the chapel. A mixture of LSD and heroin had put him into a coma. Supernaturally, he woke up by the power of the Holy Spirit, and his symptoms vanished. He came to the front and knelt in utter adoration of God.

This single healing launched ten years of harvest on the UC Berkeley campus.

The same fire that makes me contend for real miracles makes me disgusted with the fake ones. The same fire that tells me to preach a pure gospel also tells me that we are not fully preaching the gospel without miracles.

Again, read what David Wilkerson said in his sermon titled "The Fully Preached Gospel":

> The apostle Paul said to his generation: "I have fully preached the gospel of Christ" (Romans 15:19). And he described the "fully preached" gospel as one that is much more than words. It is a gospel of words and deeds! "For I will not dare to speak of any of those things which Christ has not accomplished through me, in word and deed" (v. 18).
>
> Paul was saying, "The Gentiles turned to Christ, not

because of my preaching alone, but because my words were accompanied by miraculous deeds!"

"In mighty signs and wonders, by the power of the Spirit of God, so that from Jerusalem and round about to Illyricum I have fully preached the gospel" (v. 19).

If Paul had preached and taught without signs and wonders following, his message would not have had its full impact. It would not have been the gospel fully preached! He said to the Corinthians, "Truly the signs of an apostle were accomplished among you with all perseverance, in signs and wonders and mighty deeds" (2 Corinthians 12:12).[2]

WHY GOD HEALS THE SICK

Now it is our turn to see signs and wonders. Let's start by seeing their purpose from God's point of view. Let me give you an explanation of why God heals the sick.

When T. L. and Daisy Osborn came home from India, they took a church in Woodinville, Washington. They were young and zealous to be used by God. One day Daisy announced that she wanted to hear a man of God in nearby Portland, Oregon. That man was William Branham. She went, but T. L. did not because his denomination did not endorse Branham.

Daisy returned with such a glow and joy over the miracles she saw. That did it. T. L. went and saw mighty miracles. But it was not the astonishing miracles that impacted him as much as one phrase that Branham said: "God the Father heals the sick to prove that He raised His Son Jesus from the dead."

That launched them as missionary evangelists. Now let me say that T. L. and Daisy were miracle missionary evangelists on par with Reinhard Bonnke.

I will repeat the phrase: "God the Father heals the sick to prove that He raised His Son Jesus from the dead." The Bible confirms this in Acts 14:3 (TLB): "Nevertheless, they stayed there a long time, preaching boldly, and the Lord proved their message was from him by giving them power to do great miracles."

God's miracles proved their message. That is the key. They preached the resurrection. It is our turn now, but only if we faithfully preach what God the Father will crown with miracles.

Acts chapter 4 records the first time the church was ordered to remain silent. Peter's prayer for the mission of the church to continue is illuminating because it reveals his attitude toward healing miracles. Acts 4:29–30 says, "Now, Lord, look on their threats, and grant to Your servants that with all boldness they may speak Your word, by stretching out Your hand to heal, and that signs and wonders may be done through the name of Your holy Servant Jesus."

Peter's great concern was the message. He wanted to preach it boldly and completely. He understood that miracles are the key.

It is also urgent to see that this prayer was answered in an astonishing way in the very next chapter.

> And through the hands of the apostles many signs and wonders were done among the people. And they were all with one accord in Solomon's Porch. Yet none of the rest dared join them, but the people esteemed them highly. And believers were increasingly added to the Lord, multitudes of both men and women, so that they brought the sick out into the streets and laid them on beds and couches, that at least the shadow of Peter passing by might fall on some of them. Also a multitude gathered from the surrounding cities to Jerusalem, bringing sick people and those who were tormented by unclean spirits, and they were all healed.
>
> —Acts 5:12–16

Compassion for Those in Need

The next factor in supernatural healing is compassion. Oral Roberts, T. L. Osborn, Charles S. Price, and Aimee Semple McPherson all reported being overcome by compassion for the sick. Their level of caring rose to divine heights. They agonized for the lost, the sick, and the dying. Matthew 14:14 says, "And when Jesus went out He saw a great multitude; and He was moved with compassion for them, and healed their sick." Such compassion cannot be faked. It emanates from Christ Himself. But this is not just any kind of compassion.

Spurgeon said Christ's compassion was so profound that a new word had to be invented to describe it.

> This is said of Christ Jesus several times in the New Testament. The original word is a very remarkable one. It is not found in classic Greek. It is not found in the Septuagint. The fact is, it was a word coined by the evangelists themselves. They did not find one in the whole Greek language that suited their purpose, and therefore they had to make one. It is expressive of the deepest emotion; a striving of the bowels—a yearning of the innermost nature with pity.

Then he added:

> I suppose that when our Saviour looked upon certain sights, those who watched him closely perceived that His internal agitation was very great, his emotions were deep, and then his face betrayed it, his eyes gushed like founts with tears, and you saw that his big heart was ready to burst with pity for the sorrow upon which his eyes were gazing.[3]

Identifying With Christ

This final point is the most explosive. Healing power will rest on those who make a great discovery about themselves. The key is found in 1 John 3:8: "He who sins is of the devil, for the devil has sinned from the beginning. For this purpose the Son of God was manifested, that He might destroy the works of the devil."

You are the hands of Christ extended. You are His voice raised in a dark and evil generation. But you must identify with Him totally.

You must passionately desire to destroy the works of the devil. You are a destroyer of the works of the devil!

Few understand how the anointing is a product of hatred. Hebrews 1:9 says, "You have loved righteousness and hated lawlessness; therefore God, Your God, has anointed You with the oil of gladness more than Your companions."

Alexander Dowie saw miracles after a plague struck his church in Sydney, Australia, killing many members of his congregation. An inner rage transformed him until he called out to God with a pure heart and was rewarded with so much power that it left his entire congregation free of plague.

John G. Lake saw his wife die, and it unlocked a fury against evil that swept the world with healing.

POWER ALWAYS HAS A PURPOSE

Look again at the scripture from Isaiah that Jesus read in Luke chapter 4.

> And He was handed the book of the prophet Isaiah. And when He had opened the book, He found the place where it was written: "The Spirit of the LORD is upon Me, because He has anointed Me to preach the gospel to the poor; He has sent Me to heal the brokenhearted, to proclaim liberty to the captives and recovery of sight to the blind, to set at liberty those who are oppressed; to proclaim the acceptable year of the LORD."
>
> —LUKE 4:17–19

The most powerful part of those verses is this phrase: "The Spirit of the LORD is upon Me, *because*" (emphasis added). Your *because* ruins you for all other plans, purposes, and goals. You must surrender to the one thing you are assigned to do. You must be able to list your purpose, articulate it simply and clearly, and execute it with extreme focus.

God's last-day church will go "out and [preach] everywhere; the

Lord working with them and confirming the word through the accompanying signs" (Mark 16:20). That is what God envisions for us.

I close this chapter with more of the powerful words of David Wilkerson.

> The miracles of this last-day church will be genuine, real, indisputable, undeniable—and yet they will not be well-known. Instead, they will issue forth from the hands of ordinary, holy, separated saints who know God and are intimate with Jesus.
>
> These believers will emerge from the secret closet of prayer—a small, prepared army full of faith, with no other desire than to do the will of God and glorify Him....They will be fearless against demons, casting down great principalities and powers. They will also be powerful in prayer, they'll open entire nations for the gospel. And God will confirm His Word by their mighty deeds![4]

PART IV:

FINISHING STRONG

It is not arrogant to believe we can do better in situations where others have failed. Here are the pitfalls to avoid and the secrets you must embrace to finish strong.

Chapter 18

ELIJAH'S BIG MISTAKE

E LIJAH MADE A big mistake. There is no way around it. Why should we take a look at his mistake? For a very big reason. The devil will lie back and concede that an awakening is inevitable. He waits to attack right after a great breakthrough. And that is exactly what happened to Elijah.

I wrote this book because I see what is coming. Some of it is already here. But I knew all the time I was writing that one crucial fact had to be faced. We must face the fact that taking our turn is important, but being ready for what happens afterward is just as important.

If you think I am overstating my case, consider this: Elijah called down a miracle as great as any in the Old Testament. Let's read those verses again.

> Then the fire of the LORD fell and consumed the burnt sacrifice, and the wood and the stones and the dust, and it licked up the water that was in the trench. Now when all the people saw it, they fell on their faces; and they said, "The LORD, He is God! The LORD, He is God!"
>
> —1 KINGS 18:38–39

This was the total annihilation of Baal. The perverted nation fell on its face, essentially thrown to the ground by the concussion of God's holy fire. Elijah is not just vindicated; he is unquestionably God's man. Surely, he is on his way to applying this same firepower to eradicate Ahab and Jezebel.

How is it possible that just hours after this victory of victories we find Elijah wishing he were dead? He even asks God to take his life. This is what happened:

> And Ahab told Jezebel all that Elijah had done, also how he had executed all the prophets with the sword. Then Jezebel sent a messenger to Elijah, saying, "So let the gods do to me, and more also, if I do not make your life as the life of one of them by tomorrow about this time." And when he saw that, he arose and ran for his life, and went to Beersheba, which belongs to Judah, and left his servant there.
>
> But he himself went a day's journey into the wilderness, and came and sat down under a broom tree. And he prayed that he might die, and said, "It is enough! Now, Lord, take my life, for I am no better than my fathers!"
>
> —1 Kings 19:1–4

Lesson 1: Where Elijah Went Wrong

Here is our first lesson: Elijah's expectation of the people was too high. We must be careful when we predict immediate results. Never promise a result that is conditional upon people's free will.

The only thing you can be certain of is that you will do what God said and leave the results to Him. Your fidelity to say and do what the Holy Spirit says is your only true goal and expected result.

Elijah expected a mass reformation. He was undone by disappointment because his hope was in the people's reaction. He believed he would lead the nation back to God and His ways. But much like what we saw in America after September 11, churches were filled with citizens praying, and we sang patriotic songs at all our sporting events. But it was only for a little while.

Not only did Israel not repent as Elijah had expected—he saw that he was not safe. Matthew Henry wrote,

> One would have expected, after such a public and sensible manifestation of the glory of God and such a clear decision

of the controversy depending between him and Baal, to the honour of Elijah, the confusion of Baal's prophets, and the universal satisfaction of the people—after they had seen both fire and water come from heaven at the prayer of Elijah, and both in mercy to them, the one as it signified the acceptance of their offering, the other as it refreshed their inheritance, which was weary—that now they would all, as one man, return to the worship of the God of Israel and take Elijah for their guide and oracle, that he would thenceforward be prime-minister of state, and his directions would be as laws both to king and kingdom. But it is quite otherwise; he is neglected whom God honoured; no respect is paid to him, nor care taken of him, nor any use made of him, but, on the contrary, the land of Israel, to which he had been, and might have been, so great a blessing, is now made too hot for him.[1]

Elijah panicked when he did not see the result he had expected. He should not have run. He should have realized that the cultural sin ran so deep that Mount Carmel was only the first step in restoring Israel.

He should have remembered how many were still worshipping Baal during both the drought and the famine. Likewise, we must understand that just because we get to take a turn, it does not mean the change will happen overnight.

A great evil has ensconced itself in every layer of American life. Anyone who prescribes a light touch or half a cure is part of the threat. We must, we can, and we will learn from past mistakes because the turn we take at evil must be complete and unstoppable until it removes the threat.

Look at how many in America have responded to sickness, lockdowns, and violence. Evildoers have stepped up their perversion. They have intensified their hatred of God. We cannot panic; we cannot let up. We have a long battle ahead of us.

So how do we keep from panicking and growing weary in well doing?

LESSON 2: WE CAN SUCCEED WHERE ELIJAH FAILED

The second lesson is this: it is not arrogant or disrespectful to believe we can do as well as or even better than our spiritual heroes. They would be the first to push us to do better than they did. It does good to learn from a past mistake unless you are determined to act on it. Yes, I am saying that we can succeed at a point where Elijah failed.

And how will we find the will to match or exceed our heroes? By realizing the sheer necessity of it. We have no choice! Let me explain why this is such a key to this hour. The military morale of the United States at the beginning of World War II was very low. A huge criticism was heaped on our military by other nations.

When Hitler declared war on us, we had few weapons and even fewer soldiers. There was widespread doubt that we were up to the task. So then why did we have so great a turnaround? The American will to fight became awesome. And the war machine to save freedom rose seemingly out of nothing. How did we do it?

We can offer all kinds of explanations, but the easiest is this: we had to do it.

Why, then, should we believe that we can repeat and exceed the exploits of Christian heroes who have gone before us? The answer again is clear: we have to do it.

Now we will look at another great truth that will keep us from falling short of our purpose. We must stand our ground, no matter how impossible it seems. When your early breakthrough turns into a long, drawn-out battle, you must stand.

Elijah was not supposed to run. That will be clear to us in a moment. But because he ran, evil was prolonged in the nation of Israel. Our hero did recover, and he did his duty after all. But it took an outrageous act of theft and murder for him to jump back into plan A.

The whole account is recorded in 1 Kings 21. In verse 4 we find

King Ahab angry and sulking on his bed, refusing to eat. But it doesn't take long for Jezebel to hatch a plan.

> But Jezebel his wife came to him, and said to him, "Why is your spirit so sullen that you eat no food?"
>
> He said to her, "Because I spoke to Naboth the Jezreelite, and said to him, 'Give me your vineyard for money; or else, if it pleases you, I will give you another vineyard for it.' And he answered, 'I will not give you my vineyard.'"
>
> Then Jezebel his wife said to him, "You now exercise authority over Israel! Arise, eat food, and let your heart be cheerful; I will give you the vineyard of Naboth the Jezreelite."
>
> —1 KINGS 21:5–7

She was essentially saying, "Don't worry. I'll take care of this." Then she wrote letters using Ahab's name and seal and sent them to the elders and leaders in Naboth's city. In the letters she told them to call a fast, put Naboth at the head table, and plant two false witnesses across from him who would stand up and accuse him of blaspheming God and the king. Then they were to stone Naboth to death.

In verses 11–14 we see that her plan was carried out exactly as she had ordered.

> So the men of his city, the elders and nobles who were inhabitants of his city, did as Jezebel had sent to them, as it was written in the letters which she had sent to them. They proclaimed a fast, and seated Naboth with high honor among the people. And two men, scoundrels, came in and sat before him; and the scoundrels witnessed against him, against Naboth, in the presence of the people, saying, "Naboth has blasphemed God and the king!" Then they took him outside the city and stoned him with stones, so that he died. Then they sent to Jezebel, saying, "Naboth has been stoned and is dead."

When Jezebel received the report that Naboth was dead, she said to her husband, "Arise, take possession of the vineyard of Naboth the Jezreelite, which he refused to give you for money; for Naboth is not alive, but dead" (v. 15). Ahab followed his wife's instructions and went down to take possession of Naboth's vineyard.

But the Lord warned Elijah that King Ahab was about to take possession of Naboth's field. In verse 19 He told Elijah to meet the king in that field and deliver the following message:

> You shall speak to him, saying, "Thus says the LORD: 'Have you murdered and also taken possession?'" And you shall speak to him, saying, "Thus says the LORD: 'In the place where dogs licked the blood of Naboth, dogs shall lick your blood, even yours.'"

Imagine the boldness it took to speak such words to the king's face. But Elijah did as the Lord commanded, and when Ahab asked how he found him, Elijah replied,

> I have found you, because you have sold yourself to do evil in the sight of the LORD: "Behold, I will bring calamity on you. I will take away your posterity, and will cut off from Ahab every male in Israel, both bond and free. I will make your house like the house of Jeroboam the son of Nebat, and like the house of Baasha the son of Ahijah, because of the provocation with which you have provoked Me to anger, and made Israel sin." And concerning Jezebel the LORD also spoke, saying, "The dogs shall eat Jezebel by the wall of Jezreel." The dogs shall eat whoever belongs to Ahab and dies in the city, and the birds of the air shall eat whoever dies in the field.
>
> —1 KINGS 21:20–24

The doom he was sent to bring on the house of Ahab is finally executed, but now Elijah is modeling something else for us: past failure is not an excuse to stay down. Elijah had to face his failure and exact the justice God demanded.

Ahab met death in the vivid detail of the prophet of God.

> Now a certain man drew a bow at random, and struck the king of Israel between the joints of his armor. So he said to the driver of his chariot, "Turn around and take me out of the battle, for I am wounded."
>
> The battle increased that day; and the king was propped up in his chariot, facing the Syrians, and died at evening. The blood ran out from the wound onto the floor of the chariot. Then, as the sun was going down, a shout went throughout the army, saying, "Every man to his city, and every man to his own country!"
>
> —1 KINGS 22:34–36

Jezebel also died as Elijah predicted.

> And [Jehu] looked up at the window, and said, "Who is on my side? Who?" So two or three eunuchs looked out at him. Then he said, "Throw her down." So they threw her down, and some of her blood spattered on the wall and on the horses; and he trampled her underfoot. And when he had gone in, he ate and drank. Then he said, "Go now, see to this accursed woman, and bury her, for she was a king's daughter." So they went to bury her, but they found no more of her than the skull and the feet and the palms of her hands. Therefore they came back and told him. And he said, "This is the word of the LORD, which He spoke by His servant Elijah the Tishbite, saying, 'On the plot of ground at Jezreel dogs shall eat the flesh of Jezebel.'"
>
> —2 KINGS 9:32–36

You cannot let past failure—not just yours, but the failure of the church—keep you from getting up again and again to finish your course, even if others see you in a certain light, even if they cannot imagine you as a powerful weapon against evil. You have no excuse for listening to them or for hanging around them.

Realize that some results will be delayed. But God will keep His word! You must not cut and run from your post even when it looks like your efforts have no results. Stand!

I do not doubt that we will see great manifestations of God. But I also expect withering resistance from the forces in control who will not yield their power easily.

There is certain strange relief in knowing that we have no choice but to be great for His glory. The battle for freedom is on us, and we have no deferment.

There is no other nation for you to run to. We take our stand here and now. Any other idea is just a fantasy.

The disciples of Jesus faced another case of high expectations. After Jesus rose from the dead, He appeared to them on the road.

> Now behold, two of them were traveling that same day to a village called Emmaus, which was seven miles from Jerusalem. And they talked together of all these things which had happened. So it was, while they conversed and reasoned, that Jesus Himself drew near and went with them. But their eyes were restrained, so that they did not know Him.
>
> And He said to them, "What kind of conversation is this that you have with one another as you walk and are sad?"
>
> Then the one whose name was Cleopas answered and said to Him, "Are You the only stranger in Jerusalem, and have You not known the things which happened there in these days?"
>
> And He said to them, "What things?"
>
> So they said to Him, "The things concerning Jesus of Nazareth, who was a Prophet mighty in deed and word before God and all the people, and how the chief priests and our rulers delivered Him to be condemned to death, and crucified Him. But we were hoping that it was He who was going to

redeem Israel. Indeed, besides all this, today is the third day since these things happened."

—LUKE 24:13–21

"We were hoping that it was He." They fixed their hope on a physical earthly throne and did not discern that there was a throne for Christ, but its glory was infinitely greater than what they envisioned.

The same thing holds true for you and me. We must accept the facts of our current situation, no matter how brutal they seem. We must never lose faith in the final victory.

Embrace these truths, and you will finish strong. Now *that* I can guarantee.

Chapter 19

DON'T SLOW THE TRAIN TO THROW ROCKS AT BARKING DOGS

Y OU HAVE DECIDED to make a difference. Your decision is final. Now let me warn you of one thing you must never do. You must never slow the train to throw rocks at barking dogs. Never.

Momentum is one of God's greatest gifts. The benefits of momentum are almost endless. Boiled down to its essential definition, the word *momentum* means forward motion. You must keep moving forward.

Martin Luther King Jr. said, "If you can't fly, run; if you can't run, walk; if you can't walk, crawl; but by all means, keep moving."[1]

But be warned that almost immediately after you embark on your vision, all hell will break loose. For no good reason, people will start hating you. You will be persecuted. People close to you will betray you. All this will happen to try to stop you. But again, stopping is the one thing you can never do.

The simplest way to turn your biggest crisis into your biggest opportunity is to ask yourself, "Why am I being attacked?"

It is obvious that you are a threat. But how can you be a threat? There is only one way you can be a threat: if you are God's chosen vessel accomplishing His mission. The enemy himself is admitting you are a powerful force. Remember this: the devil only attacks those he fears.

REVIVAL AND REFORMATION: DO YOU KNOW THE DIFFERENCE?

We want a new America. We want to transform the direction and condition of our nation. We will never get there if we are tricked into slowing down to respond to attacks, threats, and distractions.

Winston Churchill said it this way: "You will never reach your destination if you stop and throw stones at every dog that barks."[2]

If we want a new country, we'd better know the distinct difference between two words: *revival* and *reformation*. One is supposed to lead to the other, but it rarely does because the train almost never reaches its destination.

A revival is an outpouring of the Holy Spirit that generates repentance and mass conversions. The church wakes out of slumber and compromise, spilling out of church buildings and into a despairing world.

Reformation is the next step. The devil bitterly opposes it because of what reformation does to a culture. Here is how revival becomes reformation: those in the revival outgrow emotional experiences and seek to become like Christ. Excitement turns to discipline and a truly transformed person. Reformation becomes the conscience of a nation. It does what the word implies—it reforms.

John Wesley, who started the movement that became Methodism, did not just see revival; he saw reformation. The result of his tireless effort was a change in English law. In the last letter Wesley ever wrote, he encouraged William Wilberforce to abolish slavery in Britain, and he did. This reformation also influenced many other righteous laws in Britain. In summarizing J. Wesley Bready's *England Before and After Wesley*, Donald Drew notes that several members of parliament, governors, politicians, bankers, and businessmen were converted to Christianity as a result of Wesley's ministry. He then shows the many streams of legal transformation that flowed from them:

Peruse the lives and labours of the social emancipators during the 19th Century. There is time to mention only a few of their names: Wilberforce and Clarkson—slavery abolished; Lord Shaftsbury, Sadler—industrial emancipation; Elizabeth Fry, John Howard—prison reform; Plimsoll—ships' safety regulations; Hannah More, Robert Raikes—Sunday Schools established.[3]

Here's the thing: we don't need another book that stirs people if it has no permanent result. That is the last thing I want for this book! Again and again, we have seen movements rise and then fall away before their time and before their destiny.

I pray that you will be imbued with a perseverance that will never stop and never slow down. Having said this, let's move on to the answer of how to keep the locomotive going forward.

Four Factors That Slow the Train

Let's take a look at the four factors that will cause you to slow the train: panic, criticism, betrayal, and distraction.

1. Panic

Panic is "sudden uncontrollable fear or anxiety, often causing wildly unthinking behavior."[4] We saw the best example of this in the previous chapter.

Elijah slowed the train out of panic. He had Ahab and Jezebel dead to rights. He came so close to bringing deliverance to a nation! But he panicked. And the result was a fiery revival that did not go on to reform Israel.

Here is what *The Pulpit Commentary* says about that moment:

History tells of many great souls, hardly less brave than Elijah's, which have succumbed to a sudden panic. Anyhow, it is evident that for the moment Elijah had lost faith in God, otherwise he would certainly have waited for the "word of the Lord," which had hitherto invariably guided his movements.[5]

Notice how it says that every other time Elijah waited for the word of the Lord before any important decision. We can learn from his mistake. Let's take a closer look.

Elijah was disappointed that Jezebel was not afraid of God and the astounding miracle on Mount Carmel. This truly shocked him. But Jezebel was not afraid for a reason. It is embedded in these verses:

> And Ahab told Jezebel all that Elijah had done, also how he had executed all the prophets with the sword. Then Jezebel sent a messenger to Elijah, saying, "So let the gods do to me, and more also, if I do not make your life as the life of one of them by tomorrow about this time." And when he saw that, he arose and ran for his life, and went to Beersheba, which belongs to Judah, and left his servant there.
>
> —1 KINGS 19:1–3

Ahab did not mention God or how the fire consumed everything. He told her what *Elijah* had done. He makes it seem like Elijah performed a magic trick and then fooled the people into killing the prophets of Baal. Another clue is her reaction: "So let the gods do to me." If she had seen the astonishing way the fire fell, she wouldn't talk so easily about other gods.

2. Criticism

The Welsh Revival, 1904–1905, was one of the purest demonstrations of mass conversion and conviction of sin in modern history. One hundred thousand men were converted in Wales in a movement led by young Evan Roberts.

But harsh criticism mixed with physical and emotional exhaustion sent him on a downward spiral. He began hearing voices and doubted his ability to discern the source. He became obsessed with self-examination and was harsh toward his audiences.

Finally, a modern Jezebel, Jesse Penn-Lewis, a Welsh evangelical speaker and author, enticed him. According to Jennifer LeClaire,

Penn-Lewis seduced and deceived the revivalist in the prime of his anointing. Penn-Lewis, whose doctrine was largely rejected in Wales and is even now described as apostate teaching by some modern theologians, sought to ride on Roberts' coattails. Ironically, this Jezebel-like woman flattered him with words that aimed to ease the suffering he was experiencing from the religious spirits amid revival. But her smooth words didn't heal his soul. He suffered a nervous breakdown and went to live at this wealthy woman's home to recover.[6]

Before I say more about criticism, let me pause briefly to address fatigue. There is nothing noble or spiritual about wearing yourself out. Being physically or emotionally exhausted can make you more vulnerable to spiritual attack and temptation. It can even be prideful—the pride of thinking that everything God is doing is being done by you and cannot be done without you.

Now back to criticism. It can be lethal because of how it makes us feel. The most hurtful criticisms are the ones that attack us in the very areas we are working so hard to improve. But it is all about the feelings!

Don't believe everything you feel! Feelings are not facts; feelings are feelings. They do not always objectively represent what is taking place around you. Feelings of shame, embarrassment, frustration, anger, inadequacy, and hopelessness are based on a lie. It is hard at the moment of criticism to separate fact from fiction.

Think of it this way: there is an element of truth in almost every criticism, but that is not important right now—not if it gets you to slow the train. You might be obsessed with getting to the bottom of why a newspaper, magazine, or other media outlet said unfair and horrible things about you. Watch out! That is your subtle desire to please people.

You might also be overtaken by fear that this criticism will destroy your plans. Here is how you handle it: see the criticism as a town your train is passing through. Soon it will be behind you. Later, you can reflect on valid criticism when you are in a much stronger condition.

Finally, I do not talk to or answer any accusations from leftist media. Why would I give comments to liars? They will just twist anything I say.

3. Betrayal

Martin Luther King Jr. said, "In the end, we will remember not the words of our enemies, but the silence of our friends."[7] Betrayal is unavoidable. It is the one attack that comes out of nowhere. It is one of the last things you expect.

Why does betrayal happen? I can think of three common reasons.

First is false expectations. Read this carefully. Your closest relationships have one thing in common: expectation. When I befriend or hire someone, I must be very careful to understand what they expect of me. I ask myself, "What are they hoping to get from this relationship?"

It never occurred to me to check for this until the same form of betrayal kept happening repeatedly, making me wonder what was going on. Each time we went through a betrayal, the person would gossip to someone else about how I had broken a promise to them.

Here's the critical part: in every case, I had never ever made the promise to them. It was simply an expectation they had built up in their minds. "This is what I am going to get from knowing Mario."

That's when I realized I must be very clear, and so must you. I realized that I must ask point-blank, "What do you expect to come out of our friendship?" Or, "What do you expect to gain from working for Mario Murillo Ministries?"

Let me add quickly that this must work both ways. My close friends are not a means to an end for me. I love them, and I am devoted to being a good friend. The same goes for those who work for me.

The second common reason for betrayal is not knowing

someone's true nature. You can know someone for years and not know what they will be like in the heat of battle. We are dealing with some very hot issues. It will amaze you—when push comes to shove—how many Spirit-filled believers are in favor of abortion, transgenderism, and gay marriage.

The first time your organization is attacked for these things, those folks are suddenly unavailable. Sometimes it is not even that they believe in these immoralities; they simply don't want to fight.

The third common reason for betrayal has to do with change. You have changed. In your promotion and improvement, you are "breaking up the old gang." Your new level of zeal is not comfortable for them.

Few things hurt as badly as being betrayed. But keep moving! Winston Churchill famously said, "If you're going through hell, keep going."[8] I couldn't agree more.

I know it hurts to be betrayed, but once again, feelings are your enemy. Go ahead and feel it—but do not slow the train. You are just passing through. It might also help you to remember that while it's true some passengers will get off the train, it's also true that some better ones will jump on.

4. Distraction

Welcome to the "big daddy," the number one thing that slows a train: distraction. This book is not about martial arts, but Bruce Lee said, "It is not daily increase but daily decrease—hack away the unessential! The closer to the source, the less wastage there is."[9]

There is simply no way you can juggle what you were doing before with what you want to do now. You will have to hack away at everything unessential. Nothing will demand more courage or discipline than removing distractions from your life. It does not just demand courage but brutal courage.

Distraction can take many forms. That secure position may just be a distraction—or worse, a prison. Staying at that same desk because of your obligations is a disastrous move if it means you cannot answer the real call on your life. Money is often the worst thing to consider when you hear the call of God.

People can be a distraction. If you are a kind person, I promise you there is someone in your life who is self-invited and inappropriate in their demands on you. They mistake your kindness as weakness.

In the Old Testament, Nehemiah was constantly asked to attend meetings with people who undermined God's work. Here is how he reacted:

> Now when Sanballat, Tobiah, Geshem the Arab, and the rest of our enemies heard that I had built the wall and that there was no breach left in it, although at that time I had not set up the doors in the gates, Sanballat and Geshem sent to me, saying, Come, let us meet together in one of the villages in the plain of Ono. But they intended to do me harm. And I sent messengers to them, saying, I am doing a great work and cannot come down. Why should the work stop while I leave to come down to you?
>
> —NEHEMIAH 6:1–3, AMPC

To do the tent crusades along Highway 99 that have become so amazing, I had to do something painful. I had to stop doing conferences.

I discovered that conferences—especially the ones that have gone on year after year without change—must be guilty until proven innocent. In this climate of division and persecution of the church, it is simply too tempting to do things that have no chance of bringing America back to God.

WOWSE is an acronym for "with or without someone else." You must develop a strong WOWSE factor! It means what it says: you are determined to do what God has called you to do, with or without someone else. This train is not stopping. If others are not on board, you must keep moving, even if you must go it alone.

The dogs can be very loud. They can be very convincing. But

your mission is too great, and the stakes are too high for you to risk not reaching your destination.

CREATE MOMENTUM NOW!

Once you know your mission and your direction, start! You must create momentum as soon as possible. Do not wait until every objection is answered before you start. If you do, you will never start.

Don't get bogged down with the details of your journey or how your plans will come together. Just fire up the locomotive and watch the momentum build.

The final urgency is time. We have no idea how much time we have before freedom's torch is extinguished. We are now seeing the promise of a vast season. Whatever you are going to do, you must do now.

Jesus said, "I must work the works of Him who sent Me while it is day; the night is coming when no one can work" (John 9:4).

The devil will tell you that you are not qualified. Relatives will tell you that you are crazy to try this. Guilt, obligation, threats, and hatred will bark at you to slow down. You may not know how to do this. Do it anyway. You may not know where the money will come from. Keep rolling.

John Maxwell said, "Momentum solves 80 percent of your problems."[10] I agree with him. I believe your doubts, fears, and questions about getting to your destination can be crushed beneath the wheels if you just keep moving.

Chapter 20

IF YOU COULD HEAR JESUS PRAYING FOR YOU

A RE YOU SERIOUS about taking your turn against the evil in America? Then you better know that for the devil, it's not business; it's personal—especially if you are contesting strongholds that have been undisputed for centuries.

If you are serious, you need a formula for dealing with fear and discouragement. It would be downright foolish to cover so many topics in this book and not say anything about fear and discouragement.

The enemy of your soul cannot ignore you. He has too much to lose, and you have too much to gain. He will never leave you alone. His weapons of choice are not just fear and discouragement but *sudden* fear and discouragement. He favors shock and awe. Believe me, when you strike a blow against wickedness, you will have his undivided attention.

What should we do to be ready for these attacks? For starters, we must be aware of how intense they can be.

I mentioned how Evan Roberts fell into a sudden depression, but he's not the only example. According to Michael Reeves,

> It might come as a surprise to some that Charles Spurgeon had a lifelong battle with depression. His reputation as a famed and powerful preacher, his cheery wit, and his cigar-smoking manliness might lead us to imagine there could never be a chink in his Victorian Englishman's armor. It shouldn't be a surprise, of course: being full of life in a fallen world must

mean distress, and Spurgeon's life was indeed full of physical and mental pain.

As with Roberts, the onset of Spurgeon's depression was sudden. The attack came when he was just twenty-two years old. There he was with a big church and twin babies at home to care for when tragedy struck.

> He was preaching to thousands in Surrey Gardens Music Hall when pranksters yelled, "fire." A panic to exit the building ensued, killing seven and leaving twenty-eight severely injured. His wife, Susannah, wrote, "My beloved's anguish was so deep and violent, that reason seemed to totter in her throne, and we sometimes feared that he would never preach again."[1]

Does this sound familiar? We have mentioned Elijah's fear twice before. Just after a moment of triumph—as great as any a vessel of God had ever known—he ran for his life. We also looked at Evan Roberts, cut down by criticism in his early twenties.

A vessel of God at the apex of effectiveness suddenly struck down by fear and depression? Why do I mention these stories? Am I trying to scare you away from doing great exploits? No! Just the opposite.

I want you to learn how to triumph where those who have gone before us have failed. Remember what I said in chapter 18: it is not arrogant or disrespectful to believe we can do as well as or even better than our spiritual heroes. They would be the first to push us to do better than they did.

I have also said that revival rarely moves on to become that great and mighty miracle called reformation. Time and again, great leaders from God have been disqualified in their prime because they could not handle sudden fear and depression.

When will we break this vicious cycle? I began this book with—of all things—a baseball story. Why? Because the amazing part is not just that Kirk Gibson went up to bat; the amazing part is that he succeeded where so many before him had failed.

That is what I want for you! I want us to break the cycle of defeat and half-cures that have plagued the American church. And the only way to do it is to understand how to defeat the monsters of fear and depression that attack when you least expect them and are most likely to be destroyed.

When I say, "It's our turn now," in this chapter, I do not mean what I have said in other chapters. This message is not about it being our turn because Wokeness has made Americans miserable. I am not using the phrase here to refer to the fact that all the signs point to a great harvest.

No! I am saying something completely different here. I am saying, "It's our turn now to succeed where others have failed. It's our turn to keep going after the vicious attack. It's our turn to unlock the secret that would have kept Elijah going straight for Jezebel and kept Evan Roberts going in the great Welsh Revival."

SPURGEON DISCOVERED THE SECRET

I want you to know that Spurgeon found the answer. He learned the truth that I am about to relate to you.

Michael Reeves writes that in an 1890 sermon titled "The Tenderness of Jesus," Spurgeon spoke "while feeling his own weakness about Christ as the High Priest who feels for us in our infirmities." Spurgeon said,

> This morning, being myself more than usually compassed with infirmities, I desire to speak, as a weak and suffering preacher, of that High Priest who is full of compassion: and my longing is that any who are low in spirit, faint, despondent, and even out of the way, may take heart to approach the Lord Jesus....
>
> Jesus is touched, not with a feeling of your strength, but of your infirmity. Down here, poor, feeble nothings affect the

heart of their great High Priest on high, who is crowned with glory and honor. As the mother feels with the weakness of her babe, so does Jesus feel with the poorest, saddest, and weakest of His chosen.[2]

Spurgeon's revelation is far greater than it sounds. Why? Because he is talking about how the High Priest operates during our attacks.

I will now come out and say it! If you could hear Jesus praying for you in the next room, you would not fear a thousand enemies. The very idea of overhearing Christ speak to the Father about you should send an eternal quiver through your soul. What would you hear Him pray?

Here's why you need to know. Today's disciple faces threats that were unheard of even ten years ago. World events are explosive. Changes are dizzying. The child of God navigates a world that can be truly frightening.

Having children and grandchildren who depend on us makes it more difficult. We wonder what will happen to them. How can I protect them in such a violent and unpredictable time?

For these and many other reasons, we must have a new and unshakable relationship with God. We need faith like Daniel had in the lions' den. We need authority like the disciples had to open prison doors. We must own a walk that conquers sickness, lack, and sudden attacks.

Above all, we need to discern the works of Satan. He knows his time is short, and he has broken into a frenzy to take down as many as possible.

We can rely, to a degree, on powerful preaching. We can play worship music in our prayer rooms and quell the dismaying emotions of this time. But we need something far more. We need something so amazing that it holds us, no matter what. That, my friend, is where Jesus' prayers for us matter most.

Here are some facts about Jesus praying for you:

- He started praying for you the moment you got saved. The world can't enjoy the benefit of His prayers. John 17:9 says, "I pray for them. I do not pray for the world but for those whom You have given Me, for they are Yours."

- He will not stop praying for you. Hebrews 7:25 says, "Therefore, He is also able to save to the uttermost those who come to God through Him, since He always lives to make intercession for them." At this moment, He is lifting your situation before the Father, and that prayer is unending.

- He prayed that Satan would not touch you. In John 17:15, Jesus prays, "I do not pray that You should take them out of the world, but that You should keep them from the evil one."

- He has prayed in advance of your greatest hour of testing, just as He did for Peter. Luke 22:32: "But I have prayed for you, that your faith should not fail; and when you have returned to Me, strengthen your brethren."

Here is the most important fact of Jesus praying for you:

- He says you are His. Let's take a closer look at what that means. His love for you is not just tender; it's fierce.

Consider the mama grizzly as she snuggles her cub. She is the essence of love. Now try to come between her and her cub. The loving mom instantly becomes the most terrifying creature on earth. She will stop at nothing to protect her cub. Both the tender moment and the terrifying one are expressions of the same love.

Here's the thing: that instinct is from God. The same Jesus who comforts you with unmatched tenderness turns His wrath on the evil one when you are threatened. It would be breathtaking to see the difference between His intercession when you need comfort and when you need to be rescued from Satan's attack.

He will not let anything come between you and Him. Paul said it this way in Romans 8:38–39 (NIV): "For I am convinced that neither death nor life, neither angels nor demons, neither the present nor the future, nor any powers, neither height nor depth, nor anything else in all creation, will be able to separate us from the love of God that is in Christ Jesus our Lord."

That is why I say, if you could hear Jesus praying for you in the next room, you would not fear a million enemies.

Four Things Jesus Asked God to Give Us

John 17 has the most fully recorded prayer that Jesus ever prayed. We must look at it because it is about to do something unexpected to you. Jesus asked the Father for four things:

1. that we would be kept

2. that we might be sanctified

3. that we might be united

4. that we might be glorified

Let's look at what Matthew Henry wrote:

It was a prayer that was a preface to his sacrifice, which he was now about to offer on earth, specifying the favours and blessings designed to be purchased by the merit of His death for those that were His; like a deed leading the uses of a fine, and directing to what intents and purposes it shall be levied. Christ prayed then as a priest now offering sacrifice, in the virtue of which all prayers were to be made. It was a prayer that was a specimen of His intercession, which He ever lives to make for us within the veil.[3]

I love old-time English, don't you? You just read something so explosive that I despair of doing it justice. Henry is telling us that Jesus is laying out to the Father a clear declaration: "I am about to give My life for them. I am innocent, and My sacrifice will win great favor, grant blessings, and satisfy justice. I want them to have all the favors, blessings, and miracles that My shed blood will purchase."

But the most stunning part is when Matthew Henry says, "It was a prayer that was a specimen of His intercession, which He ever lives to make for us within the veil."

Jesus' prayer to enforce the blessings of the cross and resurrection on us did not stop there. This was just a foretaste of the prayers Jesus continues to pray for us now.

The Book of Hebrews builds and expands on what John 17 says. It compares the priesthood of Jesus with human priests.

> Also, there were many priests, because they were prevented by death from continuing. But He, because He continues forever, has an unchangeable priesthood. Therefore He is also able to save to the uttermost those who come to God through Him, since He always lives to make intercession for them. For such a High Priest was fitting for us, who is holy, harmless, undefiled, separate from sinners, and has become higher than the heavens; who does not need daily, as those high priests, to offer up sacrifices, first for His own sins and then for the people's, for this He did once for all when He offered up Himself. For the law appoints as high priests men who have weakness, but the word of the oath, which came after the law, appoints the Son who has been perfected forever.
>
> —HEBREWS 7:23–28

Think of all those years from Abraham to Jesus: the types, the shadows, the laws of the Levitical priests, and the myriad ways we saw that sin could not be atoned for by animal sacrifice. We could not have intimate fellowship with a God who could not look upon sin.

Then the desire of ages came. He paid the price once and for all and became our flawless, unending provider of blessings through His intercession.

If you could hear Jesus' voice as He prays for your strength, courage, protection, and boldness, no fear or depression could stop you. You could cross the finish line with total victory.

But there is more. To endure torture, humiliation, and death on the cross, Jesus prayed for a special miracle. "Jesus spoke these words, lifted up His eyes to heaven, and said: "Father, the hour has come. Glorify Your Son, that Your Son also may glorify You" (John 17:1).

When Jesus says *glorify* here, He does not mean "exalt Me"; He means "let Your glory rest on Me so that I will finish My course." To understand, we turn again to Matthew Henry:

> The Father glorified the Son upon earth, First, even in his sufferings, by the signs and wonders which attended them. When they that came to take Him were thunder-struck with a word—when Judas confessed Him innocent, and sealed that confession with his own guilty blood—when the judge's wife asleep, and the judge himself awake, pronounced Him righteous—when the sun was darkened, and the veil of the temple rent, then the Father not only justified, but glorified the Son. Nay, Secondly, even by his sufferings; when He was crucified, He was magnified, He was glorified, (ch. 13:31). It was in His Cross that He conquered Satan and death; His thorns were a crown, and Pilate in the inscription over His head wrote more than he thought. But, Thirdly, much more after His sufferings. The Father glorified the Son when He raised Him from the dead, showed Him openly to chosen witnesses, and poured

out the Spirit to support and plead His cause and to set up His Kingdom among men, then He glorified Him. This He here prays for, and insists upon.[4]

God put glory on Christ to carry Him through His agony. The Bible says the same thing about us in our persecution: the Spirit of glory rests on us! Look at 1 Peter 4:14, which says, "If you are reproached for the name of Christ, blessed are you, for the Spirit of glory and of God rests upon you. On their part He is blasphemed, but on your part He is glorified."

That Spirit of glory can rest on us for the same purpose it rested on Jesus: For us to be carried in the hour of our great test! To prevail when so many others have failed! We can have the courage of Daniel in the lions' den. We can prevail as the great heroes of the Bible did in their time.

Honestly, you may not like what you see when you look in the mirror. You may say you do not feel confident about taking on a great exploit. Let it go! Because someone who matters is saying things about you that are completely different from what you are saying about yourself. He is saying, "Father, give them strength and wisdom. Let them know You are with them through the fire, agony, and loneliness."

You belong in this group:

> And what more shall I say? For the time would fail me to tell of Gideon and Barak and Samson and Jephthah, also of David and Samuel and the prophets: who through faith subdued kingdoms, worked righteousness, obtained promises, stopped the mouths of lions, quenched the violence of fire, escaped the edge of the sword, out of weakness were made strong, became valiant in battle, turned to flight the armies of the aliens.
>
> —Hebrews 11:32–34

Let us break the vicious cycle of failure. Let us be the ones who kept going when everyone else stopped. Let us be the ones described in Daniel 11:32: "Those who do wickedly against the covenant he shall corrupt with flattery; but the people who know their God shall be strong, and carry out great exploits." Let it be said of us, we did not pervert or fall short of our appointed end of transforming America.

How can we succeed where others have failed? How can we break the vicious cycle and come forth as gold in the hour of testing? How can we be the ones who said, "It's our turn now!"—and did not fail?

I will say it one last time with emphasis: if you could hear Jesus praying for you in the next room, you would not fear a thousand enemies!

WHAT I WANT MOST FOR YOU IN THE WHOLE WORLD

NINETEEN-YEAR-OLD JOE WAS driving to work on Highway 99 in Fresno. He was addicted to heroin, and his liver and kidneys were failing. He knew nothing about our tent crusade. Suddenly he saw the tent from the freeway and heard a voice say, "Go and get in that tent." So he did.

He called his boss to tell him why he couldn't come to work and was fired immediately. It was 4:30 in the afternoon, so he sat in the tent for two hours, waiting for the meeting to start.

Meanwhile, as I was driving to the tent, I also heard the voice of God telling me everything you just read about Joe. All the glory goes to God. My clear instructions were, "Do not preach. Look for a young man about nineteen. You will know who he is. Tell him everything I told you about him."

As the meeting started, I spotted Joe sitting near the center aisle, three rows back. Then this happened:

"What is your name, son?" I asked.

"Joe."

"Joe, Jesus showed me you are addicted to heroin. A demonic power is being broken off you. Not only that, your liver and kidneys are being healed." Joe collapsed to his knees, sobbing.

His healing was just the beginning. He was utterly delivered and born again. Moments later he was praying out loud in an unknown tongue as Jesus baptized him in the Holy Spirit. Again, all glory goes to Jesus.

Why did I tell you this story? Because Joe's story inspired this book. Joe's miracle showed me that God is doing something most Christians are oblivious to.

Here's another example. Many people in Hanford, California, are still talking about what happened in the supermarket when one of our volunteers, a young man, was paying for his groceries. He simply said, "Jesus loves you," to the woman at the checkout counter. She immediately buried her head on the counter, sobbing.

Then there were four nights in Colorado Springs, Colorado, in July 2022. The power of the Holy Spirit was on full display, and many healings and miracles happened. Here are several I can clearly recall:

- One woman had her bones, feet, neck, back, and hands healed. She had been unable to walk without pain, yet she began running up and down in the aisles.

- Five women there had intestinal issues, and God healed them all.

- Some had issues with the neck, shoulders, eyes, dizziness, and racing heart, and God healed every one of those ailments.

- Two women who had similar pain from being in accidents were healed.

- One woman had twelve afflictions, including trouble walking and stabbing pain in the back. When she was healed, she took off running for joy.

- Another woman had a tumor, and she also needed healing in her heart, feet, and spine. God healed all of them.

Then I felt the presence of God become even more intense, so I came down from the platform and began interacting with the crowd. When I approached one man, he was healed of heart disease. Next, a woman was healed in her jaw, eyes, hip, knee, and back.

Healing after healing took place: severe pain in the body and many diseases in the heart, blood, brain, and lungs. One person was healed of mysterious throat and stomach pain.

The Lord had me call out multiple people in various sections of the tent. One section contained many who had heart and lung disease, and in another section, cancers in the stomach and esophagus. All were healed!

So many others: jaw pain, headaches, tumors, pernicious anemia, sickle cell anemia, neuropathy, dizziness, and diabetes—all healed by the power of Jesus Christ!

The Holy Spirit showed me one man who had been suffering from hemophilia, and he was healed. Then I called out to a woman sitting toward the right side of the tent. I told her she was being healed of liver and kidney disease. As she was being healed, the Holy Spirit came upon her. I said, "There is a new tongue in you. Begin to speak it out." Immediately, she began praying in the most beautiful prayer language.

I asked if anyone else in the tent had never been baptized in the Holy Spirit and never spoken in tongues. I told them, "Raise your hands and receive it!" Soon, the tent erupted with the sound of people speaking in tongues, many for the first time. I said, "You were not asking for tongues; you were asking for more of Jesus!"

The Lord gave me a scripture, Psalm 110:3: "Your people shall be volunteers in the day of Your power; in the beauties of holiness, from the womb of the morning, you have the dew of Your youth."

Why are these things happening to us? The answer is clear. God has added an extra dimension and manifestations to our outreach. Why? Because we are operating under the direct supervision of the Lord of the harvest. He directs where we go, when we go there, what we say, and when we say it.

If only I could sit with you over coffee and explain more clearly what I am so desperate to say. We are needlessly ineffective. We are powerless for no good reason. We insist on defending business as usual when we could be seeing results overnight. I want that for you so badly—more than anything in the world!

But I had to go through my own private Gethsemane. I had to die to all the accepted norms and embrace the truth of what God was doing now. It was not easy. I faced ridicule for believing so great a harvest was possible.

But my giant step of faith was still before me. It would be painful before it was glorious. I had to let God set me apart from Christianity incorporated. I was put in hiding just like Elijah.

The fire had to burn out all my fear of saying the one thing God wanted me to admit, the only thing He wanted to hear from me. Then came the blazing confession He wanted. I had to confess *it's my turn now*! Anything less would have disqualified me.

But after I said it, wow! Suddenly everything looked different. All the factors I had assumed made America hard to reach were instantly reclassified as catalysts to soul winning. All the obstacles became opportunities!

My team and I are no longer making plans; we are in a plan—a master plan! We are not in a frenzy to develop better machinery or methods. The engine that drives us is the instruction of the Lord of the harvest. We can still see the dark and wicked mess America is in, but we see it in hope, not despair.

It's your turn to ignore the critics and the threats. Do not slow the train! Keep going, remembering that it's all about the children. We must save our nation for them!

It's your turn now! It's time to act on what you have read in these pages. You must see that you belong at the table of influence. You must confess that you are a destroyer of the devil's works. You must hear Jesus praying for you in the next room. You will not cower before any Jezebel threat. You have a tongue of fire. You will not quit.

The final question is this: How will we win all these souls? That question shrinks down to size when you see what Isaiah saw—the Lord high and lifted up. The Lord of the universe wants to win souls. He is sending out a call.

The world is dying. The lost are waiting, groping in deep darkness. Let a cry rise out of you unlike any in your whole life, a cry so fierce and irrevocable that hell itself will convulse: "Here I am, Lord; send me!"

NOTES

CHAPTER 1

1. MLB Vault, "Vin Scully Calls Kirk Gibson's Legendary 1988 World Series Game 1 Game-Winning Homer (Full At-Bat)," YouTube, August 3, 2022, https://www.youtube.com/watch?v=jeGFSEIONyA.

CHAPTER 2

1. Matthew Henry, *Matthew Henry's Commentary on the Whole Bible*, ed. Anthony Uyl, vol. 2-1, *First Kings to Esther* (Woodstock, Ontario, Canada: Devoted Publishing, 2017), 83.
2. Henry, *Matthew Henry's Commentary on the Whole Bible*, vol. 2-1, 83.

CHAPTER 3

1. Abraham Lincoln, "Lincoln's Second Inaugural Address," National Park Service, March 4, 1865, https://www.nps.gov/linc/learn/historyculture/lincoln-second-inaugural.htm.
2. David Lockmiller, "New York Times Assessment of President Lincoln's Second Inaugural Address" (online symposium), January 21, 2017, https://rogerjnorton.com/LincolnDiscussionSymposium/thread-3248-post-63466.html#pid63466.
3. Abraham Lincoln, "House Divided Speech," National Park Service, June 16, 1858, https://www.nps.gov/liho/learn/historyculture/housedivided.htm.
4. Frontline, "Josephus Describes the Romans' Sack of Jerusalem," *The Wars of the Jews, Book 6*, from *The Works of Josephus*, translated by William Whiston (Peabody, MA: Hendrickson Publishers, 1987), accessed November

2, 2022, https://www.pbs.org/wgbh/pages/frontline/shows/
religion/maps/primary/josephussack.html.

5. Henry, *Matthew Henry's Commentary on the Whole Bible,*
   vol. 2-1, 83.

6. Chris Hulshof, "2 Questions to Ask Before You Quote
   Someone," Lifeway Research, February 5, 2019, https://
   research.lifeway.com/2019/02/05/2-questions-to-ask-before-
   you-quote-someone/.

7. Paul Jehle, "Pilgrims," Plymouth Rock Foundation, July 1,
   2019, https://plymrock.org/the-compact-and-declaration-a-
   united-ideology/.

8. Henry, *Matthew Henry's Commentary on the Whole Bible,*
   vol. 2-1, 83.

Chapter 4

1. Peter Marshall, "The Message of Elijah for Today," *The
   Lamplighter,* March/April 2007, 4 (reprinted from an
   audio album of the March 11, 1944, sermon "Trial by
   Fire"), http://lamblion.com/xfiles/publications/magazines/
   Lamplighter_MarApr07_Elijah.pdf.

2. Myah Ward, "Blackburn to Jackson: Can You Define 'the
   Word Woman'?," Politico, March 22, 2022, https://www.
   politico.com/news/2022/03/22/blackburn-jackson-define-
   the-word-woman-00019543.

3. Marshall, "The Message of Elijah for Today," 4.

4. K. J. Zucker et al., "Gender Dysphoria in Adults," *Annual
   Review of Clinical Psychology* (2016), 12:217-247.

5. T. S. Lee et al., "Human Fetal Tissue From Elective
   Abortions in Research and Medicine: Science, Ethics, and
   the Law," *Issues in Law & Medicine* (Spring 2020): 3-61,
   https://pubmed.ncbi.nlm.nih.gov/33950608/.

6. Greg Cannella, "Disney Removes 'Ladies and
   Gentlemen, Boys and Girls' Greeting From
   Magic Kingdom Fireworks Show," CBS News,
   July 2, 2021, https://www.cbsnews.com/news/

disney-removes-ladies-and-gentlemen-boys-and-girls-
magic-kingdom-fireworks/.

7. Lisa Kim, "Disney Opposes Florida's 'Don't Say Gay'
   Bill, CEO Says, Following Outcry Over Its Silence,"
   Forbes, March 9, 2022, https://www.forbes.com/
   sites/lisakim/2022/03/09/disney-opposes-floridas-
   dont-say-gay-bill-ceo-says-following-outcry-over-its-
   silence/?sh=7e27907f295e.

8. Henry, *Matthew Henry's Commentary on the Whole Bible*,
   vol. 2-1, 94.

CHAPTER 5

1. Jana Harmon, "C. S. Lewis on the Problem of Pain,"
   C. S. Lewis Institute, September 1, 2012, https://www.
   cslewisinstitute.org/resources/c-s-lewis-on-the-problem-of-
   pain/.

2. Blaise Pascal, *Pensees* (New York: Penguin Books, 1966),
   75.

3. Vladimir Lenin, "The Goal of Socialism Is Communism,"
   Brainy Quote, accessed October 26, 2022, https://www.
   brainyquote.com/quotes/vladimir_lenin_136421.

4. Kerri Nelson, "The COVID-19 Labor Shortage," The
   Society for Human Resource Management, July 19, 2021,
   https://advocacy.shrm.org/wp-content/uploads/2021/07/
   SHRM-Research_The_Employment_Picture_Comes_Into_
   Focus.pdf.

5. Ayn Rand, *Atlas Shrugged* (New York: Penguin Group US,
   2005), 230.

6. John Fea, "The Secular Front in the US," Aeon, January
   22, 2016, https://aeon.co/ideas/is-secular-progressivism-
   undermining-us-democracy.

CHAPTER 6

1. John Daniel Davidson, "The Transgender Movement Is Not Just Intolerant. It's Barbaric and Violent, and It's Coming for Your Children," The Federalist, August 19, 2022, https://thefederalist.com/2022/08/19/the-transgender-movement-is-not-just-intolerant-its-barbaric-and-violent-and-its-coming-for-your-children/?.

2. Amanda Prestigiacomo, "Award-Winning Drag Queen, LGBTQ Youth Adviser Charged With 25 Counts of Child Pornography," The Daily Wire, July 6, 2022, https://www.dailywire.com/news/award-winning-drag-queen-lgbtq-youth-adviser-charged-with-25-counts-of-child-pornography.

3. Leah Hall, "Central Pa. Drag Performer Charged With 25 Counts of Child Pornography, Police Say," Fox 43, June 24, 2022, https://www.fox43.com/article/news/crime/central-pa-drag-queen-harrisburg-chambersburg-anastasia-diamond/521-6f0177c5-82e1-4ad9-8d2a-09ab36d31bc3.

4. Kristan Hawkins, "Planned Parenthood Isn't on the Way Out, It's Transitioning to Gender-Bending," The Federalist, September 6, 2022, https://thefederalist.com/2022/09/06/planned-parenthood-isnt-on-the-way-out-its-transitioning-to-gender-bending/.

5. Kelsey Koberg, "Blog Post on Teachers Union Website Claims Parents 'Make It Their Job to Undermine' Teachers," Fox News, August 12, 2022, https://www.foxnews.com/media/blog-post-teachers-union-website-claims-parents-make-job-undermine-teachers.

6. Hannah Grossman, "AFT Union Promotes Method for Teachers to Help Kids Change Their Pronouns Without Parents Knowing," Fox News, August 10, 2022, https://www.foxnews.com/media/aft-promotes-method-teachers-help-kids-change-pronouns-without-parents-knowing.

7. Kelsey Bolar, "War on Parents: Male Teacher Asked This Mom's 11-Year-Old 'Transgender' Daughter to Sleep in Boys' Cabin," The Federalist, August 10, 2022, https://thefederalist.com/2022/08/10/war-on-parents-male-teacher-asked-this-moms-11-year-old-transgender-daughter-to-sleep-in-boys-cabin/.

8. Bolar, "War on Parents."

9. Steve Peoples, "More Than 1 Million Voters Switch to GOP, Raising Alarm for Democrats," June 27, 2022, PBS News Hour, https://www.pbs.org/newshour/politics/more-than-1-million-voters-switch-to-gop-raising-alarm-for-democrats.

10. Libby Emmons, "Public Library Deletes Pictures of Drag Queens Fondling Children at Story Hour," The Federalist, July 22, 2019, https://thefederalist.com/2019/07/22/public-library-deletes-pictures-drag-queens-fondling-children-story-hour/.

11. Kristine Solomon, "Fashion Brand Under Fire for Children Modeling Bikinis on the Runway," Yahoo! News, July 18, 2016, https://sg.news.yahoo.com/fashion-brand-under-fire-children-000000859.html.

12. Lindsey Tanner, "Trans Kids' Treatment Can Start Younger, New Guidelines Say," AP News, June 15, 2022, https://apnews.com/article/gender-transition-treatment-guidelines-9dbe54f670a3a0f5f2831c2bf14f9bbb.

CHAPTER 7

1. "The Importance of Being Ethical, with Jordan Peterson," Hoover Institution, recorded April 20, 2022, posted on YouTube, April 29, 2002, https://www.youtube.com/watch?v=DcA5TotAkhs.[2] Matt McGregor, "Leftist-Turned-Conservative Podcasters Unapologetically Question Pervading Progressive Ideologies," The Epoch Times, August 21, 2022, https://www.theepochtimes.com/leftist-turned-conservative-podcasters-unapologetically-

question-pervading-progressive-ideologies_4676156.
html?welcomeuser=1.

Chapter 8

1. David Wilkerson, "End Time Values," World Challenge, accessed November 2, 2022, https://www.worldchallenge. org/end-time-values.
2. The Leopards, "File: Grave Stone of John Newton.JPG" (photo), Wikimedia Commons, March 25, 2010, https:// commons.wikimedia.org/wiki/File:Grave_stone_of_John_ Newton.JPG.

Chapter 9

1. Peter Faustino, "Nothing Is More Powerful Than an Idea Whose Time Has Come," *Policy Matters* (blog), National Association of School Psychologists, October 2, 2019, https://www.nasponline.org/research-and-policy/policy-matters-blog/nothing-is-more-powerful-than-an-idea-whose-time-has-come#:~:text=Victor%20Hugo%20is%20 the%20French,minds%20being%20open%20to%20ideas.
2. *Merriam-Webster*, s.v. "kairos," accessed September 26, 2022, https://www.merriam-webster.com/dictionary/kairos.

Chapter 10

1. Ron Eggert, comp., *Tozer on Christian Leadership* (Camp Hills, PA: WingSpread Publishers, 2001).

Chapter 12

1. Katie Reilly, "'Action Is the Only Remedy to Indifference': Elie Wiesel's Most Powerful Quotes," *Time*, July 2, 2016, https://time.com/4392252/elie-wiesel-dead-best-quotes/.
2. Thomas Paine, "The Crisis," The Independence Hall Association, December 23, 1776, https://www.ushistory.org/ paine/crisis/c-01.htm.

3. Matthew Henry, *Commentary on the Whole Bible,* ed. Ernie Stefanik, vol. 3, *Job to Song of Solomon* (Grand Rapids, MI: Christian Classics Ethereal Library, 2000), 893.

4. Eric Metaxas, *Bonhoeffer Bible Study Guide: The Life and Writings of Dietrich Bonhoeffer* (Nashville: Thomas Nelson, 2014), 59.

CHAPTER 13

1. Andrew Mark Miller, "North Carolina Gay Pride Event Slammed Over Video of Young Child on Stripper Pole," *New York Post*, August 25, 2022, https://nypost.com/2022/08/25/north-carolina-gay-pride-event-slammed-over-video-of-young-child-on-stripper-pole/.

2. Carson Williams, "Gender Identity Development Theory: Critiques and New Perspectives," *The CSJE Blog*, February 15, 2018, https://acpacsje.wordpress.com/2018/02/15/gender-identity-development-theory-critiques-and-new-perspectives-by-carson-williams/.

3. *New Oxford American Dictionary, Third Edition*, s.v. "parent" (New York: Oxford University Press, 2010), 1273.

4. *Merriam-Webster*, s.v. "parent," accessed September 26, 2022, https://www.merriam-webster.com/dictionary/parent.

5. Ian Prior, "Parents, Here Is Your Back-to-School Checklist to Combat Wokeism at Your Child's School," Fox News, August 20, 2022, https://www.foxnews.com/opinion/parents-back-to-school-checklist-combat-wokeism-childs-school.

6. "America First Legal Outs Another PA School District for Violating First Amendment Rights, Blocking Parent's Access to Disturbing Woke Materials, Demands District Reveal Class Curriculum," America First Legal, August 31, 2022, https://www.aflegal.org/news/america-first-legal-outs-another-pa-school-district-for-violating-first-amendment-rights-blocking-parents-access-to-disturbing-woke-materials-demands-district-reveal-class-curriculum.

7. Prior, "Parents, Here Is Your Back-to-School Checklist to Combat Wokeism at Your Child's School."
8. Anna Bartlett Warner, "Jesus Loves Me, This I Know," Hymnary.org, accessed October 28, 2022, https://hymnary.org/text/jesus_loves_me_this_i_know_for_the_bible.

CHAPTER 15

1. R. Arthur Mathews, *Born for Battle* (Robesonia, PA: Overseas Missionary Fellowship, 2004), 12.
2. E. M. Bounds, *The Complete Works of E. M. Bounds on Prayer* (Grand Rapids, MI: Baker Publishing Group, 2004), 338.

CHAPTER 16

1. Kyle Swenson, "Black-Clad Antifa Members Attack Peaceful Right-Wing Demonstrators in Berkeley," *Washington Post*, August 28, 2017, https://www.washingtonpost.com/news/morning-mix/wp/2017/08/28/black-clad-antifa-attack-right-wing-demonstrators-in-berkeley/.
2. Lisa Feldman Barrett, "When Is Speech Violence?," *New York Times*, July 14, 2017, https://www.nytimes.com/2017/07/14/opinion/sunday/when-is-speech-violence.html.

CHAPTER 17

1. David Wilkerson, "The 'Fully Preached' Gospel," World Challenge, November 18, 2011, http://davidwilkersontoday.blogspot.com/2011/11/fully-preached-gospel.html.
2. Wilkerson, "The 'Fully Preached' Gospel."
3. Charles Spurgeon, "The Compassion of Jesus," The Spurgeon Archive, December 24, 1914, https://archive.spurgeon.org/sermons/3438.php.

4. David Wilkerson, "God's Vision for the Last-Day Church!," World Challenge, accessed November 2, 2022, https://www.worldchallenge.org/gods-vision-last-day-church.

CHAPTER 18

1. Matthew Henry, *Commentary on the Whole Bible*, vol. 3.

CHAPTER 19

1. All-powerful Motivation, "If You Can't Run Then Walk/Martin Luther Motivational Speech," YouTube, March 17, 2017, https://www.youtube.com/watch?v=MFOFs0iAwDg.
2. Terence M. Dorn, PhD, *Quotes: The Famous and Not So Famous* (London: Page Publishing, 2021).
3. Donald Drew, "England Before and After Wesley," Disciple Nations Alliance, accessed September 26, 2022, http://disciplenations.org/wp-content/uploads/2020/04/England-Before-and-After-Wesley_Drew.pdf.
4. *New Oxford American Dictionary, Third Edition*, s.v. "panic" (New York: Oxford University Press, 2010) 1266.
5. Henry Donald Maurice Spence Jones, Joseph S. Excell, "Commentary on 1 Kings 19," *The Pulpit Commentary* (Peabody, MA: Hendrickson Publishers, 1985).
6. Jennifer LeClaire, "How Jezebel Killed One of the Greatest Revivals Ever," God TV, March 11, 2021, https://godtv.com/how-jezebel-killed-one-of-the-greatest-revivals-ever/.
7. Darryl Lezama, *From the Civil Rights Pioneers to the First African American President and Beyond* (Bloomington, IN: Author House, 2014), 47.
8. Geoff Loftus, "If You're Going Through Hell, Keep Going—Winston Churchill," *Forbes*, May 9, 2012, https://www.forbes.com/sites/geoffloftus/2012/05/09/if-youre-going-through-hell-keep-going-winston-churchill/?sh=491990b7d549.

9. Bruce Lee, *Striking Thoughts: Bruce Lee's Wisdom for Daily Living* (North Clarendon, VT: Tuttle Publishing, 2015), 190.
10. Les Parrott and Leslie Parrott, *Strengthen Your Marriage: Personal Insights Into Your Relationship* (Grand Rapids, MI: Zondervan, 2021), 1.

CHAPTER 20

1. Michael Reeves, "Did You Know That Charles Spurgeon Struggled With Depression?," Crossway, February 24, 2018, https://www.crossway.org/articles/did-you-know-that-charles-spurgeon-struggled-with-depression/?.
2. Reeves, "Did You Know That Charles Spurgeon Struggled With Depression?"
3. Matthew Henry, *Matthew Henry's Commentary on the Whole Bible*, vol. 5, *Matthew to John* (Grand Rapids, MI: Christian Classics Ethereal Library, 2000).
4. Henry, *Matthew Henry's Commentary on the Whole Bible*, vol. 5.